Throws and Takedowns
for sambo, judo, jujitsu and submission grappling

Throws and Takedowns
for sambo, judo, jujitsu and submission grappling

By Steve Scott

Turtle Press   Santa Fe

THROWS AND TAKEDOWNS FOR SAMBO, JUDO, JUJITSU AND SUBMISSION GRAPPLING. Copyright © 2008 Steve Scott. All rights reserved. Printed in the United States of America. No part of this book may be reproduced without written permission except in the case of brief quotations embodied in articles or reviews. For information, address Turtle Press, PO Box 34010, Santa Fe NM 87594-4010.

To contact the author or to order additional copies of this book:
call 1-800-778-8785 or visit www.TurtlePress.com

Cover photo by Jorge Garcia

ISBN 978-1-934903-08-7
LCCN 2008034781
Printed in the United States of America

10 9 8 7 6 5 4 3 2 1 0

Warning-Disclaimer

This book is designed to provide information on specific skills used in the sport of sambo, also known as sombo. It is not the purpose of this book to reprint all the information that is otherwise available to the author, publisher, printer or distributors, but instead to compliment, amplify and supplement other texts. You are urged to read all available material, learn as much as you wish about the subjects covered in this book and tailor the information to your individual needs. Anyone practicing the skills presented in this book should be physically capable to do so and have the permission of a licensed physician before participating in this activity or any physical activity.

Every effort has been made to make this book as complete and accurate as possible. However, there may be mistakes, both typographical and in content. Therefore, this text should be used only as a general guide and not the ultimate source of information on the subjects presented here in this book on sambo or any skill or subject. The purpose of this book is to provide information and entertain. The author, publisher, printer and distributors shall neither have liability nor responsibility to any person or entity with respect to loss or damages caused, or alleged to have been caused, directly or indirectly, by the information contained in this book.

Library of Congress Cataloguing in Publication Data

Scott, Steve, 1952-
Throw and takedowns for sambo, judo, jujitsu and submission grappling / by Steve Scott.
   p. cm.
ISBN 978-1-934903-08-7
1. Hand-to-hand fighting, Oriental. 2. Wrestling. 3. Mixed martial arts. 4. Martial arts--Holding. I. Title.
GV1112.S4525 2008
796.815--dc22
                      2008034781

Acknowledgements

Thanks to the following people for appearing in the photos used in this book: Ken Brink, Scott Brink, Dillon Brink, Becky Scott, Warren Frank, John Saylor, Ken Cabean, Chris Heckadon, Sean Watson, Bryan Potter, Alan Johnson, Eric Millsap, Mark Lozano, Kirk Quinones, Corinna West, Josh Henges, Jarrod Fobes, Bob Rittman, Drew Hills, John Zabel, Derrick Darling, Kyle Meredith, Kevin Green, Chris Bartley, Mike Thomas, Kolden Dawson, Mike Hallman, John Ingallina, Keith Karnisky, Nikolay Zolotukhin, Roman Zhukov, Chad Ender, Chuck Klasing, Ben Goehrung, Trevor Finch, Brian Greene, Chris Garlick, Roy Coble, Chas Owen, Will Cook and Sam Penhallow. Photos were taken at Welcome Mat and the Barn of Truth. Steve Scott, Mark Lozano, Jorge Garcia, Kent Teel and Sharon Vandenberg took photos for this book.

Contents

Introduction   9

Section One: Core Skills   13
Giving Credit Where It's Due   15
Control and Force   16
What Makes a Throw or Takedown Work   18
Controlling and Breaking Balance   20
The Four Stages of a Throw   23
Function Dictates Form   25
Safety in Throws and Takedowns   26
Training and Drilling on Throws   27
Importance of Gripping and Tie-Ups   28
The Difference Between a Throw and a Takedown   51
Effective Use of Postures, Stance and Hip Distance   51
Physical Fitness for Throwing   58
A Good Defense Can Win Fights   58

Section Two: Lifting Throws   67
The Buck   70
The Buck (No Jacket)   76
Buck Counter to Sweeping Hip Throw   80
Buck Counter to Opponent's Leg Jam   84
Buck Outside Thigh Sweep (Lift)   88
Inside Thigh Lift   91
Inner Thigh Throw to Inside Thigh Lift   95
Front Thigh Lift from Looping Grip   98
Outer Thigh Sweep   102
Foot Prop from Looping Grip   104
Thigh Sweep Throw   108
Belly-to-Belly Throw   112

Section Three: Pick Ups and Leg Grabs   115
Cuban Leg Grab (No Jacket)   118
Cuban Leg Grab (Using Jacket)   120
The Metz   124
Front Double Leg with Thigh Lift   129
Hand Prop Throw   131
Ankle Scoop Pick Up Throw   134
Ankle Pick to Toehold   137
Tight Waist and Crotch Lift   141
Hand Wheel   146

Section Four: Knee Drop Throws   151
1-Arm Knee Drop (Pulling with Sleeve)   162
1-Arm Knee Drop (Pulling with Lapel)   165
Open Opponent's Base and Attack with Knee Drop   169
Shoulder Grip Knee Drop   172
Cross Arms Knee Drop   175
Lapel and Sleeve Swing Knee Drop   180
Both Sleeves (Arm In) Knee Drop   184
Both Sleeves (Arm Out) Knee Drop   187

Both Arms Knee Drop	190
2 on 1 Lapel Knee Drop	193
Tight Waist (Hip Throw) Knee Drop	196
Back Grip Knee Drop	198
Looping Grip Knee Drop	200
Head and Arm Knee Drop	203
Arm Wrap Knee Drop	205
Face First Knee Drop	208
Fireman's Carry	212
Fireman's Carry Front Drop	216
Fireman's Carry from a Cross Grip	218
Fireman's Carry Shoulder Shoot	221
Fireman's Carry Knee Drop	226
Section Five: Leg Hooks and Sweeps	**231**
Cross Body Outer Hook (No Jacket)	234
Cross Body Outer Leg Hook (Lapel and Back Grip)	236
Cross Body Outer Leg Hook (Double Lapel Grip)	239
Sweeping Hip Throw	241
Side Sweeping Hip Throw	244
Outer Hook from 2 on 1 Tie Up	246
Outer Hook from an Overhook	250
Inner Thigh Throw (High Collar Grip)	252
Inner Thigh Throw (Attack Opponent's Leg)	256
Inner Thigh Throw (Lapel and Back Grip)	260
Inner Thigh Throw from an Overhook	262
Inner Thigh Roll to Leglock	265
Outer Leg Hook Against Opponent's Stiff Arms	269
Hopping Outer Leg Hook	272
Cross Grip Major Outer Hook	276
Minor Inner Hook	278
Minor Inner Hook from a Shoulder Throw	282
Minor Outer Hook	285
Minor Outer Hook with a Leg Grab	288
Major Inner Hook and 2 Arm Tackle	289
Hopping Major Inner Hook from a Cross Grip	292
Change Direction Inner Leg Hook	295
Foot Kick Throw	298
Section Six: Body Drop and Over Body Throws	**301**
Body Drop (Hook Opponent's Head)	304
Both Hands Body Drop	306
Open Chest Body Drop	308
Back or Belt Grip Body Drop	311
2 on 1 Far Lapel Body Drop	313
Side (Arm Trap) Body Drop	314
Back Grip Hip Throw	318
Steal Shoulder Hip throw	320
Knee Body Drop	322
2 on 1 Body Drop Front Takedown	325

INTRODUCTION

Throwing an opponent, whether it's in a sport combat situation or in a self-defense situation, proves to him that he's in over his head (literally and figuratively). The act of throwing an opponent to the ground or mat shows dominance over him and the harder you throw him, the less likely he wants to continue to fight you.

It takes skill and a lot of practice to manipulate your body and the body of a resisting opponent so that you can throw or take him to the mat with control and force. Learning how to throw someone takes concerted effort and a real dedication to learning. Usually, the "learning curve" on throwing is a lot longer than on groundfighting. This, of course, is a generalization, but generalizations are often what they are because it's the case more often than not.

This book is about functional, performance-based throws, many of which come from the tradition of Russian sambo, but the content of this book isn't strictly sambo. Any source of sport combat that has developed effective throws and takedowns are used as a basis of information. Function dictates form and beauty is in the eye of the beholder. The major goal of this book is to present functionally effective and efficient throws and takedowns that have proven themselves successful in a variety of grappling and combat sports for a variety of athletes. This is what I mean when I say "performance-based" throws and takedowns—how effectively the move works for you and the ratio of success when you use it. The more often it works for you against resisting, fit, skilled and equally matched opponents, the more effective it is for you.

This book features the throws and takedowns that people in all combat sports have come to recognize as sambo. However, throws that are used in judo, jujitsu, various styles of wrestling and submission grappling are featured as well. One of the purposes of this book is to introduce some throws and takedowns that aren't commonly presented, along with others that are; but in the end, what is presented is the compact, explosive and functional application of how to throw an opponent. I offer my point of view on the subject of functional, performance-based throws and takedowns and show what's worked for my athletes and what I've seen work for other athletes on mats in all levels of competition in a variety of fighting sports for many years. Some of the spectacular (and effective) pick-up and lifting throws seen in sambo and international judo are examined on the following pages, but this book isn't intended to simply show throwing skills because they are sensational. The skills in this book have proven their worth, and as a result, have proven the worth of the men and women who used them, on mats all over the world for a long time in a variety of combat sports.

As you will see, not every "type" of throw is presented in this book. I've tried to focus on several generic types of throws and examine each of them closely. The reason for this is simply as a matter of personal preference on my part and not to discount the value of any other type of throw or takedown. Likewise, the throws selected for presentation in this book are useful, practical, effective and interesting and all based on sound principles.

Another purpose of this book is to present a serious study of defense and how to avoid being thrown. It's my belief that a good defense can, and will, win matches. If your opponent doesn't score points on you, you're still in the fight. As my friend John Saylor has said, "A good part of winning is not getting beat."

A pragmatic approach (both in theory and in application) to throws and takedowns will be presented on these pages. While this author is far from being the ultimate authority on sambo, judo or jujitsu theory and technique, it's hoped that this book provides a practical and technically sound resource about the functional and performance-based throws used in combat sports.

It is my belief that a good throw is a good throw, no matter where (or how) you learned it. If it gets your opponent on the mat or ground with force and control and works for you on a consistently successful basis, then it's a good throw. Maurice Allen, the World Sambo Champion who introduced me to the sport many years ago, told me "Make your technique work for you." Maurice was also a world-class judo man and wrestler and when we discussed throwing techniques in judo, he gave me the same advice, only in a specific sense. He told me "Make your judo work for you." In other words, for a throw (or any technique) to be consistently successful for you, you have to make it fit you, much in the same way you tailor an item of clothing. What I mean is that for any technique, whether it's a throw, armlock or pin (or any skill), mold it so that it works for you and works for you on a consistent basis. By the same token, not every throw or takedown may work for you. You'll only find out by training hard and training smart and making a real effort, both physically and mentally, to learn as many techniques as possible, then paring them down until you find what works best for you. Also, what may not work for you now, may work at a later stage of your career. If you take the time to learn the correct fundamentals of throwing (or any phase of grappling), then you will be better able to determine how to make your technique work for you.

What may seem to be "power" throws or moves presented in this book are, in both theory and application, completely the opposite. The throws and takedowns shown on these pages all result from effective and efficient use of body mechanics, principles of breaking an opponent's posture and balance and correct use of body position and movement. All effective throws are plyometric in nature; thus, they are "power" movements by the very definition of the concept. These throws are the compact, functional and explosive result of effective gripping methods, applied use of body space, tempo, movement and position.

Being able to throw an opponent goes a long way in making you a "complete" grappler. If you've read my other books emphasizing groundfighting and submission techniques, you know that I am an advocate of taking an opponent to the mat or ground and engaging with him. Having said that, knowing how to throw effectively is a major part of getting your opponent to the ground with a consistently high ratio of success. Many proponents of groundfighting say that most fights end on the ground or mat. That's true and I agree with that statement. However, it's also true that most fights start standing up and if you know how to get your opponent to the ground with control and force, you have a much better chance of finishing him on the ground. It's my belief that no athlete should limit himself, so being able to fight or compete standing up is as fundamentally important as being able to fight or compete on the ground. Also, if you throw him to the ground hard enough, you can end the fight right then and there. So then, a throw or takedown is the initial link in a chain of events that control an opponent or adversary from start to finish. Throwing or taking your opponent to the mat or ground is the start, and successfully securing a submission technique or pin is the eventual finish in many cases.

The photographs in this book feature the athletes and friends of the Welcome Mat Judo, Jujitsu and Sambo Club. We purposely use photos taken during hard workouts in an attempt to demonstrate that the best way to get good at any phase of grappling (in this case, throws and takedowns) is to do it on the mat. As any coach or athlete knows, good points on technical matters pop up in conversation while engaged in the activity, and it's hoped that some of these small (but important) points are brought out in the pages of this book. As always, many thanks are due to the athletes and coaches at Welcome Mat, as well as the athletes and coaches with the Shingitai Jujitsu Association for their help in the making of this book. My wife Becky deserves much credit for her technical advice and editing efforts. Also, I want to offer Cynthia Kim and the professionals at Turtle Press my thanks for their support and professional advice in the development and publication of this book. This book is one of several in a series that I have written and Turtle Press has published on the subject of grappling. This series of books have covered armlocks, strangles and chokes, leglocks, pins and breakdowns, and now throws and takedowns. Turtle Press has also published my books on drill training for grapplers and my introductory book on sambo's groundfighting techniques. Please use this book as a good source of information and as a springboard for new ideas and concepts. As said before, a good throw is a good throw no matter who does it, where it's learned or what it's called; no matter if you throw your opponent in a sambo match, a judo match or in a street fight.

As a coach and author, I hope you find this book useful, regardless of what fighting sport or activity you engage in, whether it's sambo, judo, sport jujitsu, submission grappling, MMA or any form of self-defense or personal combat training. I also hope this book is a positive addition to the body of knowledge that already exists and opens new doors of thought and practical information.

Throws and Takedowns

SECTION ONE:
Core Skills

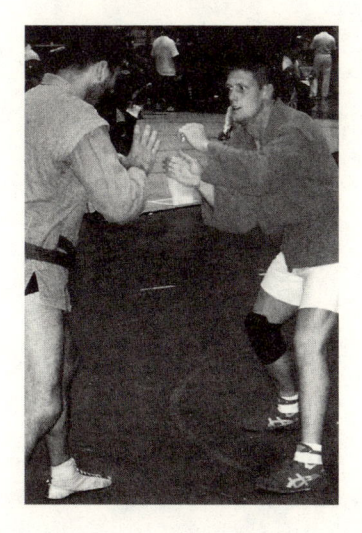

"Sometimes you have to play for a long time to be able to play like yourself."

Miles Davis, Jr.

Throws and Takedowns

GIVING CREDIT WHERE IT'S DUE

While the premise of this book is sambo's functional approach to throws and takedowns, a great deal of credit should go to the historical roots of this approach. This historical root is Kodokan Judo and Prof. Jigoro Kano. The theoretical and practical basis that Kodokan Judo established in 1882 (and in the intervening years since) has no rival. No form of grappling on earth has done more than Kodokan Judo in the development and refinement of throwing techniques. The concepts of manipulating another human being's movement that Prof. Kano established many years ago are still as mechanically viable today as they were when he taught them himself. Kodokan Judo's acceptance of new ideas and skills has created a fertile ground for the development of different techniques from a variety of different cultures. A major strength of judo is its ability to assimilate many different influences from a variety of other grappling and fighting styles. The fact that judo is an Olympic sport has done much for the technical development of all hybrid grappling sports (sambo included) and has given sports like sambo an international stage to demonstrate its functional approach to grappling and throwing.

While Kodokan Judo has done an enormous amount in the building of a foundation and its continued development of throwing techniques, the approach that the Soviets took toward a functional, performance directed type of throw changed the sport (but not entirely the physical education aspect) of judo a great deal. Not only did it change judo as a sport, it changed how we view throwing techniques in all areas of sport combat and self-defense. When sambo athletes representing the Soviet Union first appeared on international judo mats in 1962, their approach to throwing and groundfighting was viewed as radically different than the accepted range of throws and holds of Japanese origin in judo. To the trained eye of a judo athlete or coach, the throwing techniques of sambo differ (radically, in some cases) from the throwing techniques of judo generally. However, a good throw is a good throw and many throwing techniques taught in sambo look identical to their judo counterparts.

The Soviet sambo wrestlers didn't approach judo the way the Japanese did. The sambo men didn't train to perfect a technique, as was the accepted Japanese (and world) view of judo. Instead, these sambo men trained to become proficient with techniques in a variety of situations. Emphasizing utility over aesthetics, they molded the technique to work for them and had no qualms about changing a move to suit their purposes. Results were more important than the process. This isn't to say that the sambo approach to throwing is superior to the Japanese. It's simply different, and in fact, is an extension in the development of Japanese judo as an international sport. This extension of development carries on, and as sambo has been exported to other countries, it has changed and adapted as well in a similar way sport judo has. This is the premise of this book; the historical approach of accepting, adopting and adapting any throw (no matter it's origin) that works and works with a consistent ratio of success. A successful throw is a successful throw, no matter if you use it in a sambo match, a judo match or in a self-defense situation.

CONTROL AND FORCE

Two primary actions make up a successful throw. They are: (1) Control and (2) Force. These two principles (and actions) work together to create a successful throw.

Control

If you want to throw an opponent, you have to control his body first. A lot of attention will be paid to this as you read on, but it's vital to understand that if you don't control him, you won't throw him. Think of control as a series of things linked together to create the situation that ultimately results in slamming your opponent onto his back. Your first point of contact is your grip. How you grab him, grip him or tie up with him often dictates how you will throw him. Along with your grip, how you stand (your stance) is an important factor in how you throw him. Your stance and your body position in relation to your opponent are fundamental in the link of actions that make up a throw. How far your body is from his and how you are standing is all part of the sequence of events in a throw. These actions often lead to your body movement and how you control your opponent's body movement. All the actions in this sequence of events result in controlling your opponent's balance and ultimately how you position yourself into the throw, and ultimately how you attack (throw) your opponent, then follow him to the mat.

I believe it's also important to understand what is called "accelerating control or force." Basically, you're building up a good head of steam with a series of linked movements or attacks and eventually throwing him. In many cases, you will attack your opponent with another move to either fake him out to make him move a specific way, or you actually try a throw and it fails, and you use another throw that eventually throws him. This series of linked movements, often called combinations or continuation attacks is a series of throws or feints that create movement and momentum into your throw. It's often a good idea to shoot a hip or leg to open your opponent up or make him move a particular direction as a set up for a throw. Then again, some of the best (and most successful) attacks are direct and to the point, but every successful throw is a culmination of a series of things that come together at the right time and the right place against the right opponent.

If you remember that P (Position) + M (Movement) = C (Control), you will have a good formula for how to successfully control your opponent so you can throw him. This is true for any phase of grappling or fighting, but especially true when it comes to throwing an opponent. You're fighting someone who is on his feet and can move, and as a result can either attack you or defend against your attack. Your position and the position your opponent is in are vital to the execution of a successful throw or takedown. Often, how you move and how your make your opponent move, dictates both your position and his position. You have controlled the situation and can effectively throw your opponent when you've been able to control both your opponent's position and movement as well as your own. Now, how you go about doing that takes some study and a lot of hard work on the mat. That's what I'll cover on the following pages.

Remember, function dictates form and good body mechanics are fundamental to making any throw work effectively. Once you have mastered the basic movements of the technique, you can then develop it to fit your body, style of fighting and other factors. Make the throw work for you. Don't limit yourself in any way other than what the rules of your sport allow. If you have to adapt a technique to work for you, do so. Also, how you grip your opponent is vital to the success of the throw. Make it a point to experiment with the many ways of gripping the jacket or uniform and of using tie-ups without the use of a jacket or uniform to make the throw work best for you.

This entire book is actually dedicated to controlling your opponent. How well you control him determines how well you throw him.

Force

Force is how hard (or how soft) you throw your opponent and is the culmination of the sequence of events that have controlled him so that your throw is successful. Force is the result of control. When looking at the value of any throw, the two factors that determine its success are control and force. Later in this book, the difference between a throw and takedown will be discussed, but the end result of a good throw is force. The harder you throw him, the more starch you will take out of him and the less likely he will want to fight you after he's been thrown. A good throw sets up a good ground attack so don't hesitate to follow your opponent to the ground to secure a submission technique, hold him with a pin or follow up with a ground and pound attack (in MMA or self-defense).

WHAT MAKES A THROW OR TAKEDOWN WORK

Not every throw is for everybody. It's takes a lot time and effort to find the throws that work best for you, and then mold them to work for you in a variety of situations. Also, a throw that may not work well for you now, may work well for you several years from now. We all change and you may find that with the physical, mental and emotional changes we make as athletes and people, we may find success in a throw or takedown in the future that we never thought possible. Another important thing to think about is not to limit yourself to a particular throw or type of throws simply because of your size. What I mean to say is that many heavyweight athletes get locked into the belief that they have to do "heavyweight throws." Sure, it's true that some throws simply don't work all that well for some people based on body size or type, but don't hesitate to give them a try and, if you believe you have a proclivity for a particular throw, see how it can work best for you. Likewise, some people naturally tend to throw over one side than the other. Most people learn throws where they throw over their right side (right hip, right leg and so on), but don't limit yourself to only one side. You may normally be a right-sided thrower, but there may be some throws that you do well or better on the left side. The only way to find out is to experiment in practice and see what works for you.

Finding the best throw or throws is much like finding a good spouse. Something clicks. The Japanese have a good saying; "You have to feel your judo." There's that kinesthetic feeling and awareness that goes beyond the cognitive thought process.

A throw is a weapon. The action of throwing another human being down to the ground or mat is a ballistic movement. You can use it and it can be used against you. It's much like a gun in that sense. Like any other tool or weapon, it has no personality or life of it's own and how you use it is up to you. If you go into a gunfight with a .22 caliber handgun and your opponent has a .44 Magnum, you may be in trouble. But, if you're more willing to shoot and know how to shoot that .22 straighter, faster and more accurately than your opponent does his .44 Mag, you might come out the winner in that gunfight. Sure, it sounds kind of silly to compare a throw to a gun, but bear with me for a little while.

I compare the caliber of a gun's bullet to the training you put into your throw. The more powerful the bullet, combined with a rifle barrel on the gun means that gun will shoot with its full ballistic effect. If you've done your speed/strength training so that you have tremendous plyometric strength when performing the throw, then you have a .44 Magnum bullet. But if you haven't put in the physical effort, then you're only shooting a .22 caliber bullet. If you've gone to the shooting range and practiced both smart and hard, and know how to handle that handgun in realistic situations, then you're most likely going to shoot both accurately and fast, and have the stopping power, when in a real gunfight. But, if you've only shot the gun a few times and not under realistic situations, then you'll most likely not shoot very straight or fast enough when you need to. I think you get the analogy by now. It takes a combination of physical fitness training along with lots of serious training on the mat to have the explosive power and technical ability to throw an opponent in a real situation.

One more thing; when you throw your opponent, you "project" him over your own body. You don't simply lock him onto your body and fall down, but rather, lock him onto your body, then lift or elevate him up and over (or around) it, throwing him to the mat or ground with force. When you throw him backward, you don't simply drive him down, but rather, upend him with control in the direction you wish, thus creating more force and accuracy in the throwing action. Often, your opponent's body moves at different speeds when he's thrown. His upper body and lower body often move at different speeds in the actual throwing action. An example is a foot sweep where you move your opponent and sweep his feet out from under him (his feet and lower body are now moving at a faster speed than his upper body). When you perform a Knee Drop throw, you drop to your knees under your opponent's center of gravity and force his upper body to fall over your body at a faster rate of speed than his lower body. Often, in a good knee drop, your opponent's upper body is traveling forward at a fast speed before his feet even leave the mat. This is what I mean when I say you "project" your opponent over your body in a throwing motion.

With all that being said, let's look at the mechanics of a good throw. But remember, as said before, a throw or takedown is a tool and utilitarian in nature. It's like any other weapon. It's only effective if it works for you and works for you when you need it to work for you.

CONTROLLING AND BREAKING YOUR OPPONENT'S BALANCE

Controlling and breaking your opponent's balance is a combination of a lot of things that happen in a sequence (but in a fast and controlled sequence) of events. While against an unresisting partner, the only action necessary is to pull your opponent up onto his toes and attack him, but breaking the balance on a resisting, skilled and fit opponent takes more thought and effort.

When you "break" your opponent's balance, it's because you've controlled the grip or tie-up, the space between your body and your opponent's body, the movement of both your body and his body and the momentum into the direction of the attack. Sometimes, it can be a subtle movement on your part but more often; your throwing attack is a result of a relentless, explosive body movement on your part resulting in a throw. Often, "little things" become "big things." What I mean is that a minor or slight movement on your part can set in motion a series of events that can result in a throw. The better you are able to control and create the "little things" the better you are at throwing your opponent.

When you're controlling or breaking your opponent's balance, it's best to do it as you move him. It's easier to control him when he's moving or stepping than if he's firmly planted on both feet. Also, break his balance to a corner or at an angle usually. Judo uses what is known as "happo no kuzushi" or the eight directions of unbalancing. These are the 8 directions you often break your opponent's balance; front, back, right side, left side, right-front, left-front, right-rear and left-rear. Most sambo coaches I know also use this concept of unbalancing your opponent in 8 directions.

Core Skills

Using Your Lead Hand to Pull

Corinna is using her left hand to pull on Kirk's right sleeve as she fits in for a throw. Notice how she has turned her left hand upwards as if she were looking at the face of a wristwatch on her left hand. Doing this twisting motion with her pulling or lead hand tightens up the jacket on Kirk's right sleeve and controls him better. This also gives Corinna more pulling power to throw Kirk over her body and not merely lock Kirk's body onto her body. Corinna is using the standard "pull" with her left lead hand and it's a very effective way of controlling your opponent's arm and shoulder to throw him.

You Don't Always Have to Pull to Break His Balance

Chad is using his left hand to push Brian's right elbow and arm in to control and break his balance. This "squeezing together" of Chad's left hand on Brian's right elbow and his right hand and arm (on Brian's left shoulder and back) works well in controlling Brian's balance and posture. Chad can attack with a throw from this position.

Trapping His Arm to Control Balance

Alan is trapping Chuck's right elbow to his body with his left hand and controlling the situation. By trapping your opponent's arm to his body, you control his posture and break his balance. Alan can shoot in for a throw or takedown from this position.

Steer Him to Control Balance and Movement

Trevor is using his right elbow to "steer" Bryan. Trevor has firm control of Bryan's belt and has his right forearm on Bryan's back as shown. Trevor is pulling Bryan in the direction of his right elbow and into the direction and movement of the throw. By steering with your arm, hand and elbow, you can better control your opponent in most every throwing situation.

THE FOUR STAGES OF A THROW

The next four photos show the four basic stages of a throw. Remember, these 4 parts work together as a whole and the end result is control and force; they blend together. Kodokan Judo developed the concept of Kuzushi (controlling your opponent's balance), Tsukuri (building the throw or preparing to attack; fitting in for the throw) and Kake (attacking or executing the throw). These three stages of a throw really can't be improved, except to add a fourth stage; the follow through or finish of the throw to make sure he lands where and how you want him to.

Controlling (Breaking) Balance

It's often said, and rightly so, that to effectively throw your opponent, you must break his balance first. In all my years of training, competing, coaching and years spent thinking about all of this stuff, the concept of what the Japanese call "Kuzushi" or breaking the opponent's balance, is one of the hardest skills to master in judo, sambo, jujitsu or any form of martial arts training. While writing this book, I was fortunate to get the thoughts of Jim Bregman, one of the most successful judo athletes to ever represent the United States, on this subject. Jim threw a great many world-class judo (and sambo) athletes during his illustrious career and he's a legitimate expert on throwing. Jim's thoughts on breaking an opponent's balance are, "Kuzushi is the description for the 'sum total' of movement. One's entire body through grip, posture, and body space, opponent's reaction and movement (ballistic and momentum) creates the 'perfect storm.' I was always taught that your 'first attack' was the beginning of a relentless series of moves that gave you the initiative and forced your opponent into a reactive mode. As your opponent reacts to your 'onslaught,' you simply adjust your attacks to his actions and keep the momentum ratcheting up until your opponent is physically exhausted, mentally confused, or, simply unable to react out of bewilderment to your aggressive combinations and counters, relentless aggressiveness, and, single minded focus. As the pressure mounts, you accelerate the initiative you have gained and launched by your 'first attack' and the opponent crumbles, mentally and physically, landing with full force and control flat on his or her back with you firmly in control for a pin. The opponent asks, 'What happened' or 'What was that?' You don't really care because you are now fully focused on your next match!"

Throws and Takedowns

Building the Throw (Fitting In)

Ken has controlled Scott's movement and is actually fitting his body into position so he can make the throw happen. As you can see from this photo, Ken is sweeping his right thigh and starting the throw. In the same way a house is built, the foundation (unbalancing) comes first, and then the actual construction of the throw takes place. This stage is the actual construction of the throw.

Execution

The third stage of a throw is to actually attack and throw your opponent. Your body is fully committed to throwing him and the action of the throw. This photo shows Scott in the air with Ken in full control of him.

Follow Through

Ken plants Scott flat on his back with control and force and can finish Scott on the ground with a submission technique, hold-down or any move he wishes. In the same way a golfer swings through after hitting the ball off the tee or a baseball pitcher follows through after delivering a fastball, the momentum you have created in throwing your opponent requires a complete follow through to produce the best results.

FUNCTION DICTATES FORM

As said in the introduction, beauty is in the eye of the beholder. The purpose of a throw or takedown is to get your opponent to the mat or ground with control and force. Not only that, you want to be able to do it on a consistently successful basis. How you do that is up to you. Sure, there are specific ways to position your body and the body of your opponent so that specific techniques take form and shape. There are certain techniques that any trained eye recognizes as a specific throw. For instance, anytime you throw your opponent over your body with your legs split wide, that's what is recognized generally as a Body Drop throw (Tai Otoshi in Japanese). But, how you make that Body Drop throw work for you on a consistent basis is up to you. Take the basic form of the throw, seriously study how it works best and why it works in that way, and then replicate that movement so that it becomes instinctive behavior. Mold it to make it work for you. Drill on it so that you can do it without thinking. Often, when you've thrown an opponent in a match you may have to ask someone "What did I throw him with?" You instinctively got your grip, moved him into position and slammed him, then don't remember a thing about how you did it. The Japanese say that a good technician "feels his judo." In other words, he has a keen, finely tuned kinesthetic awareness that goes beyond defining in words.

Use your physical size to your advantage. Use what physical gifts the Good Lord blessed you with, and with additional training, increase those gifts. If you're tall, with long arms and legs, develop throwing skills that work best for you. If you're short, follow the same advice; make the throw or takedown work for you.

Adapt the move so that it works best for you and your body type rather than trying to force your body to do something that it's not meant to do. I'm not saying throw away the correct mechanics and fundamental movement of the technique. What I'm saying is that you must learn the correct fundamentals of the throw, making sure that it's mechanically sound and actually works, then mold that technique to fit you, your needs and the needs of what you want it to do for you. When you mold the technique to work for you on a consistent basis with a high ratio of success, that is "skill." Skill is the practical application of technique.

Also, some techniques seem more natural to some people than others. We're all different and, in many cases, a particular throw or type of throw seems more "natural" to you than others. If this is the case, go with it and try to develop that throw so that it works for you in real situations. Give it a while and take the time to see if that throw is a good one for you. In the end, it may or may not be something you can use now, but you may keep it on the back burner and use it later in your career.

Don't be a poser. In other words, don't think you have to perform a throw (or any move) a certain way simply because of the way it's supposed to look. Going back to the Body Drop throw; some athletes use a very wide split, while others use a narrower split of the legs. Some split directly in front of an opponent, while others shoot one leg to the side of an opponent. Generically, it's the same throw, but different athletes perform it under different circumstances, and in the end, it works for each of the people who use it.

SAFETY IN THROWS AND TAKEDOWNS

Knowing how to fall and land on the mat safely is important. Using crash pads is also an important part of safety in training. During the course of a normal workout, you'll take a lot of throws. Knowing how to land safely every time is vital to your well-being. Also, when you practice throwing with a partner who is confident, relaxed and can take a good fall, you will perform your throw better. Having good partners in training, and being a good partner in training, is important in developing well-executed throws and takedowns (as well as any phase of grappling or fighting). If you haven't learned how to fall safely, make sure you learn good breakfalls before attempting any of the skills presented in this book.

TRAINING AND DRILLING ON THROWS

It's not easy learning how to master a throw. It takes a lot of time and effort, both on and off the mat. As a coach, I personally believe that learning how to throw may be the hardest part of learning sambo, jujitsu or judo for most athletes. If you want quick results and don't have much patience, either develop the patience necessary and put the work and effort into developing throwing skills or figure you better try another sport that doesn't require as much time and effort. Doing countless, countless repetitions of uchikomi and full throws can be boring, and just plain hard work (both for you and your training partners). Working on the grip fighting and body movement drills can be repetitious and dull, but if you want to throw opponents with a high ratio of success, the time and effort is necessary for success. The skills presented in this book all work, but what makes them work is your dedication to developing them on a high level and making them work for you. Once you've decided what throw(s) work best for you, you then must devote countless hours on the mat on molding that throw to become an instinctive behavior. In addition to lots of mat time, develop the physical skills necessary for throwing. You need explosive power and quick foot speed, so make sure you spend a lot of time in the weight room and other places where you can develop the physical attributes necessary for throwing opponents. The harder, and smarter, you work, the better you will be as an athlete.

The use of uchikomi (fitting practice) as part of your drill training is vital to the development of good throwing skills. Uchikomi is a "rehearsal" for actually throwing someone. In my book DRILLS FOR GRAPPLERS, I have numerous uchikomi drills that can help you develop your throwing skills. I also recommend that you throw a lot on the crash pads to develop the full range of the entire throw from start to finish. Crash pads are essential for developing powerful, effective throws. Another phase of developing good throwing skills is to think about your throw(s). Analyze why your throw isn't working, or if it is working, understand why it works and translate this thought process onto the mat to repeat the successful movements that make the throw work. My good friend Harry Parker used to say, "Think about your judo, so you can feel your judo." In other words, if you put enough time and effort (physically, mentally and emotionally), it will become second nature to you; and not only second nature, it will become a big part of you and what you are.

I cannot emphasize the importance of doing lots of grip fighting drills as a regular part of your training. A good throw is an extension of a good grip and it is vital to develop skilled, aggressive grip fighting. Whether your sport is one that uses a jacket (as sambo, judo and jujitsu do) or not (wrestling or submission grappling) knowing how (and being able) to control the grip and tie up are extremely important. A common trait of all athletes who are good throwers is that they are good grippers as well. I recommend that at every practice you do several rounds of hard, aggressive grip fighting and "grip randori" where you fight your partners in a grip contest. You can do this without a jacket and try to get the best tie up.

IMPORTANCE OF GRIPPING AND TIE-UPS

Your first actual point of contact with an opponent is how you grab him and how he grabs you. In every throwing or takedown technique, how you grab your opponent dictates the success of the action. Whether you and your opponent are wearing a jacket or are in a "no gi" situation, the better you control your opponent with your grip, the better you throw him. An important point to remember is that if you don't grip or tie up your opponent well, you most likely won't throw him very well either. Before you can control your opponent's posture, movement or other aspects of throwing him, you must have a grip that works for you. Your throw often flows directly from your grip or tie up and this is why it's vital that you have good gripping skills if you want to be able to throw opponents with a high ratio of success. There are three primary gripping situations. They are:

Neutral Grip. You and your opponent are on even terms and have a lapel/sleeve grip. This is taught to beginners so they have freedom of movement and can work on equal terms when learning new throwing skills. For recreational practice or learning purposes, this is the ideal grip to start with. This is a neutral grip and gives neither fighter the advantage. I recommend learning the basic, core throws from the neutral grip initially. After you have learned the fundamental mechanical skills of the throw, adapt your grip to one that will work best for you in the way you want to use the throw.

Dominant Grip. When fighting an opponent, your goal should be to dominate the gripping situation and control his movements as much as possible. You can assert yourself as well as nullify his movement and attacks with an aggressive, dominant grip. You want to fight him on your terms, not his. This is the grip that you want to impose on your opponent so you can set him up for your throw. You may work the same throw from different grips, but each of these grips works well for you on the same throw from a different situation. You have to experiment with your grips during your workouts to find the grip(s) that work best for you in realistic situations.

Defensive/Counter Grip. If your opponent has managed to dominate or control the grip or how you grab each other, you must work to defend yourself and counter with your own grip. Do everything you can to avoid fighting on his terms. Practice lots of grip fighting or pummeling drills with a variety of training partners so you can adapt to as many grips as possible and learn how to counter them with your own grip and body movement.

Any grip that works for you with a good to high ratio of success is a good grip. In most cases, the throw you choose to use is designed from the grip that you control your opponent with or counter with. Knowing the many ways to grip, grab, manipulate and control your opponent's jacket, belt, pants, shorts, head, shoulders, arms, hands, legs or any body part or any part of his clothing is essential to knowing how to apply an effective throw. Remember, everything is a handle to grab your opponent with.

Using your hands to grab your opponent is the primary way of connecting your body to his, but you should learn how to use your arms, elbows, shoulders, hips and any part of your body possible to control him. Generally, is you are a right-handed thrower, your right hand/arm is the "steering hand/arm" and your left hand/arm is the "leading hand/arm." The Japanese consider the right hand the "tsurite" or "lifting hand" and the left hand the "hikite" or the "pulling hand." If you think of your grip on your opponent's jacket in the same way you would think of wrapping a belt or rope around him, you have a good concept of how to control your opponent with your grip. If you successfully control your opponent's grip, you are "tying him up" with the grip, controlling and breaking his posture, controlling his body movement, controlling the tempo of the action and ultimately, controlling how you throw him to the mat. Your grip is the first link in how you throw your opponent. Your posture, and your opponent's posture, is part of how you grip with him and dictates the type of throw you will choose to attack or counter with. The space between your hips and your opponent's hips dictates the posture and often dictates how you will choose to grip fight with him.

Rules of Grip Fighting

1. Immediately after you start the fight or match, or when starting after any break in the action, hold your hands up at chest level with your palms facing your opponent so that you pretend you are looking at your opponent through a television screen or picture frame. This is a good ready posture and you are prepared to attack and defend.

2. Always try to get your hands on your opponent first and get the dominant grip. Don't fight on his terms and don't let him have the better grip or tie up. Be aggressive in getting your grip. How you grip fight or fight for the tie up not only puts you in a position to attack him better, but it lets your opponent know you mean business. You're there to fight, not play. Your initial contact with your opponent is that grip. Be the one who takes control and dictates the terms of the fight.

3. If you can't get the dominant grip, try to break his grip and counter with your own grip or tie up. If you can't counter and get the dominant grip, at least get a neutral grip.

4. If you have to initially be in a neutral grip or tie up situation with your opponent, work hard to dominate the grip. You want all the odds in your favor and a neutral grip gives him as good of a chance to throw as you have of throwing him.

5. Your grip should lead to something. Use your grip or tie up to set your opponent up for your throw or takedown. Your throw flows naturally from your grip. Make sure the grip you use works best for the throw you want to use.

6. Try not to let your opponent get both hands on you. If he's a 1-handed fighter, he can't control you as well.

7. Never, ever grab with the same hand as your lead leg. In other words, if you lead with your left leg, don't grab your opponent initially with your left hand. Instead, if your lead (sugar) foot or leg is the left one, reach with your right hand to get your initial grip. This way, you're not off-balance and allowing your opponent to foot sweep you or attack you with another throw or takedown.

8. Use your steering hand as "radar." If you are a right-handed fighter, try to use your right hand to feel your opponent's movements, whether your right hand is on his lapel in the middle of his chest, on his back or shoulder; really anywhere that you can feel his movement. I used to train with a guy who was a left-handed fighter and he liked to keep his left hand planted on his opponent's chest; right in the middle if he could. He told me that this was his "radar" and he could feel if his opponent turned, even slightly.

9. Neutralize your opponent's steering hand. If he's a right-handed grappler and wants to get his right hand on you, grip it first and keep it pushed down and away from you so he can't get his hand on you. This ties in with making him a 1-handed fighter.

10. Emphasize your steering hand. If you are a right-handed fighter, this is your right hand. Use it to control your opponent. Your left hand would then assist in getting the grip, pulling him, fending off his hand, or any variety of uses. Some coaches call this the "power" hand, but I prefer to call it the steering hand because you literally steer your opponent with it.

11. I'm not fond of getting the thumb caught in the opponent's lapel. This often leads to a "floating elbow," the malady that happens when a fighter attacks with a right-sided throw and his right elbow goes up in the air, often with the right wrist bent and ineffective. By getting your thumb stuck in your opponent's collar at his neck, you are limiting yourself in how you attack and defend.

12. Shoulders over hips and lower your levels with your legs; this means that your shoulders should be directly over your hips with a straight back and good posture. Don't bend forward with your butt sticking out and your shoulders leaning for-

ward (this puts your body off-balance forward). If you have to get lower than your opponent or like to fight from this position, lower your level with your legs and don't bend forward at the waist.

13. Your weight distribution should be 50/50 most, or all, of the time. Try to have your weight distributed evenly and don't place too much weight in your heels. Don't be "heavy footed" and try to stay on the balls of your feet. Be graceful and don't plod.

14. Here's an old rule, but one that still works; don't cross your feet. You're asking to get thrown or taken to the mat. Not only that, you're off balance when you cross your legs or feet and you can't attack or defend quickly.

15. Once you get attached; stay attached to him so you can achieve a throw or takedown. If you need to change your grip, don't let go unless he's beaten you to the grip and is controlling you and you have to break free and re-grip.

16. Always use two hands to control or attack your opponent's one hand. In other words, if your opponent comes in to grip with you and leads with his one hand, it's easier to deflect his one hand with your two. You can counter-grip more effectively using both hands when possible. A good example is for you to "kill" your opponent's right hand lead. You grab his hand with both of yours, then when you pull it down to neutralize it, you can adjust your counter-grip and get the grip useful to you.

17. Avoid moving directly backward or running forward directly to your opponent. Moving directly back or forward is too easy for your opponent to throw you. By moving back in a straight line or backing away from your opponent, you appear to be passive and the referee may penalize you for it. Don't back up; instead try to move on angles and if you have to move to avoid him, try to move laterally.

18. If you break your opponent's grip or tie up, don't back up or back away. This is perfect time to re-grip or counter grip and take the offensive. If you back away as you and your opponent lose grip of each other, it appears passive to a referee.

19. Use your head as a wedge to break the grip, if necessary. Sometimes, you may have to bury your head on your opponent's chest, shoulder or even his arm and use it as a wedge to open up the distance between your bodies. You may even use your head to shuck your opponent's grip on your collar or lapel, or use your head to duck under your opponent's arm or shoulder to get to the outside. You can even wedge your head on your opponent's head or neck to gain an advantage. Rene Pommerelle used to call using your head this way your "third arm."

20. Don't get saddled thinking that you can only grip with a neutral grip (or the head and arm, or collar tie-up). While this is the basic grip used to learn new

throwing skills with, remember it's only one of the many ways you can grip or tie up an opponent. Don't fall in love with a grip for any reason other than it works and is the best to use to throw an opponent. Be willing and prepared to change grips to suit the situation.

21. This is the most important rule of grip fighting; any grip that works (and is allowed by the rules of your sport) is good.

Commonly Used Grips and Tie Ups

Here are some common grips, tie-ups and gripping situations seen in sambo, judo, jujitsu and submission grappling. Not all grips or tie-ups are shown here, but these are favorites of mine and I've seen them used often and with good success. Remember, your grip often dictates what throw you will use, so practice gripping drills and grip fighting so you are confident and skilled in grips and tie ups.

Throughout this book you will see how your grip or tie up establishes what throw or takedown you will use. Think of the grip as the first link in any throwing action. Don't hurry in and attack your opponent with a throw before getting a good grip or hold on him first. One of the best ways of making a particular technique work best for you is to find which grip works best and how to work your throw in from that grip, or you can take it from another approach and decide on your favorite throw and develop a grip to suit the needs of getting into that throw with good success. Some grips don't suit some throws, so you'll have to experiment which grip works best for you and for your throw. Often, the grip or tie up dictates how you move your opponent and how you move, as well as the space between your bodies and other factors in making any throw a success. Knowing how to grip and fight for the grip you want to use is vital in any grappling or fighting sport. There are many ways to grip or tie up with your opponent, using the jacket or not using the jacket. The grips and tie-ups shown on the following pages are a few of the commonly used grips in sambo, judo, jujitsu and submission grappling. Don't hesitate to experiment with your grips and ties ups and find out for yourself what works best for you.

Hands Up (Keep Your Guard Up)

Always have your hands up and be ready to grab or deflect your opponent's hands, arms, shoulders, chest or any part of him you need to manipulate him and control him. In the same way a boxer keeps his guard up so he can hit his opponent and block his opponent's punches, grapplers must have their hands up. Have your hands up near shoulder level, open as shown in this photo, and pretend you are looking through a television screen. Keeping your hands up will enable you to use them freely to attack and defend. Both John and Will have their hands up, ready to attack or defend as necessary.

Neutral Grip

The neural grip, called "kumi kata" in judo is a standard grip and excellent for learning the basic skills of most throwing techniques. This grip (initially developed by judo's founder, Prof. Jigoro Kano) allows both people to attack and defend freely, giving neither an advantage. He designed the grip in this way to allow this free exchange of techniques. Both Eric and Jarrod have their right hand on the opponent's right lapel at the chest and their left hands on the opponent's left sleeve at just above the elbow. This gives each athlete a hold on both the right and left sides of his partner. Many grapplers use this neutral grip as part of their grip fighting set of skills as it can accommodate many types of throwing attacks. This is not a dominant grip, and doesn't give either athlete the advantage. This is why we call it a neutral grip.

Open Your Opponent's Chest

Eric is attacking Jarrod from a neutral grip. You can see how Eric is "opening up the chest" of the opponent. When you open up your opponent's chest, you are using your hands and arms to snap open his jacket and jacking his arms up and away from his body so you can hit in with a throw. In the same way you would use your right hand to cast out a fishing rod, Eric has used his right hand to snap Jarrod's left lapel out. Look at Eric's right forearm jammed directly on Jarrod's left pectoral area and Eric has his right hand holding onto the lapel. Eric's right hand is pointing up and his right elbow is pointing down and slightly out to control Jarrod's entire left side. Eric's right arm, elbow and hand are steering Jarrod into the direction of the throw. As he does this, Eric is using his left hand to lift and pull on Jarrod's right sleeve just above the elbow. Doing this "opens" Jarrod's chest and allows Eric the room to fit in for his throw.

Back Grip (Monster Grip)

Bryan is using his right hand to reach over the shoulder of Drew in what is known as the back grip (also called the monster grip by many judo athletes). By grabbing Drew in this way, Bryan is closing the space between the bodies and has a firm, solid grip on Drew's entire upper body. Many forward throws in sambo use this grip. Bryan would use his right hand to "suck" or steer Drew into the direction of the throw as he uses his left hand to pull. Bryan's hands work together, although performing different tasks, in the action of breaking Drew's posture and moving him into the throw. In this way, we envision a belt or rope connecting Bryan's right and left hands, giving him control of Drew's body.

Here's another photo of the back grip in a situation that happens often in sambo and judo. Chad has his right arm over Brian's left shoulder and back and is using his left hand on Brian's right sleeve to pull Brian in for as much control as possible. I call this "killing your opponent's shoulder" and it's a good way to set him up to throw him. Chad is successful breaking Brian's posture and setting him up for a throw. Chad has grabbed Brian's belt and is controlling him with it. You can use his belt or jacket in the back grip to control your opponent better.

Belt Grip

Your opponent's belt is a perfect handle and you should use it if possible. That belt is wrapped around his body and you can use it to lift or manipulate him. It may not always be possible to grab his belt, and if you can't you can grab the jacket as shown before.

Shoulder Grip

A common grip used in many throws is the shoulder grip as shown by Josh in this photo. Josh moved his right hand around Nikolay's left upper arm just below the shoulder and is grabbing Nikolay's jacket strongly. This is a preferred grip to the back (monster) grip if you are shorter than your opponent or the same height and can't reach over his back.

Lapel and Shoulder Grip

Josh is using his left hand to grab Nikolay's right lapel at chest level as he uses his right hand for a shoulder grip. This is a good grip, allowing Josh a lot of freedom of movement and the ability to attack to Nikolay's front, to Nikolay's rear or across Nikolay's body.

Pretend You Have a Belt in Your Hands Wrapped Around Your Opponent

As Josh attacks Nikolay with a Sweeping Hip throw, pretend Josh has wrapped a belt or rope around Nikolay from one hand to the other. By using your hands to pull and steer your opponent into the direction of the throw, you are using the concerted effort of both hands, and at the same time each hand has a specific function. Envisioning a rope looped around and controlling your opponent when you think of gripping is a good way to actually control your opponent's body better. It doesn't mater what grip you use, if you pretend you have a belt or rope stretched from one hand to the other, you will use your hands more efficiently and effectively.

Looping Grip

This is a variation of the back grip, and Bryan is using his right hand to reach over Drew's right shoulder as shown in this photo. This is a strong grip, tying up Drew's right side and is often used in sambo.

Here is the looping grip in action. Steve has used his right hand and arm to reach over Drew's right shoulder and has attacked Drew with an Outer Hook throw. You can see the control Steve has of Drew's entire right side.

2 on 1 Shoulder Grip

It always a good idea to use both of your hands to isolate and work on your opponent's one side, shoulder or arm. Steve is using both of his hands to control Brian's right shoulder and entire arm. In the sport of judo, you have to immediately attack your opponent after establishing this grip, but in sambo and most other grappling sports, you can get this grip and use it to control your opponent.

Both Lapels Grip

Steve is grabbing each of Roy's lapels with each of his hands and using the lapels to steer Roy. This is a useful grip and gives Steve the edge by controlling the inside grip. Controlling the grip from the inside like this often keeps your opponent from using his arms effectively, but more important, if gives Steve better control of Roy's shoulders.

Both Sleeves Grip

Mark is gripping each of Kirk's sleeves with each of his hands. This is an excellent grip and can be used with many throws. It's really your choice where you grab along your opponent's sleeves.

Pistol Grip

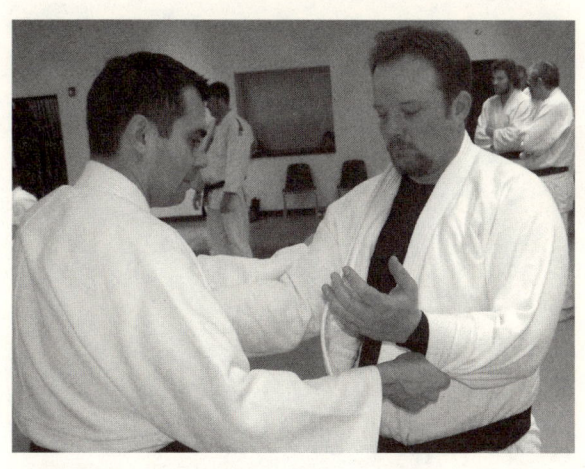

Kirk, on the left, has used his right hand to grab the very end of John's left sleeve. Kirk is gripping the flap of John's sleeve in the same way he would grab a pistol grip. This controls the entire arm and is useful for many throws.

Russian 2 on 1 Grip (No Jacket)

Keith, on the right, has John in a Russian 2 on 1 tie up or grip. The Russians use this tie up in all styles of grappling and use it as a set up for many throws and takedowns. It's a great way to manipulate your opponent, and is used in many situations. Many throws and takedowns in sambo use the 2 on 1 and the cross grip (a variation of the 2 on 1) and this grip or ties up is a distinguishing feature of sambo. You will see this type of grip used for a variety of throws and takedowns in this book. Experiment with how you can use this grip to work the throws and takedowns you now use.

Russian 2 on 1 Grip (Using Jacket)

One of the key features of sambo is the Russian 2 on 1 grip. Ken is using this popular grip on Scott to bend him over and break his posture to set him up for a throw or takedown. This is a great way to control your opponent and force him to be a one-handed grappler. Using the 2 on 1 grip with a jacket gives you another handle (the jacket) to control your opponent better.

Cross Grip

The cross grip is a variation of the Russian 2 on 1 grip. Will, on the right, is using his left hand to pull John's left hand across his body and to Will's left hip for control.

Cross Grip (No Jacket)

John has cross-gripped Mike and is attempting to control Mike's left arm more so that he can work the cross grip into a Russian 2 on 1 grip and control Mike's entire left side. Mike is using his right hand to push against John's head to create space and break away from John's cross grip.

Shoulder Trap (Underhook)

Alan has used his right hand and arm to hook under Chuck's left shoulder and trapped it. Look at how Alan is pulling down with his right hand on the top of Chuck's left shoulder and is using his head to trap the left shoulder and upper arm. Alan also controls the body space by using his left hand to push on Chuck's head.

2 on 1 Far Lapel Grip

Ken has shot in for a Body Drop throw and has used his right hand to grab Scott's right lapel. As he does this, Ken is pulling on Scott's right sleeve to throw him.

2 on 1 Near Lapel Grip

Steve is using both of his hands on the left lapel of Brian to set him up for a throw. Remember, any grip that works for you and is allowed in the sport you are fighting in is a good one!

Tight Waist

Anytime you reach around your opponent's hips and control them with your arm, this is a "tight waist." You can see how Alan has used his right hand to control Chuck's hips and has hooked his right hand on Chuck's right hipbone for control. This is a good way to lock your body to your opponent's body for more control and to close the space to set him up for a throw or takedown.

Body Lock and Overhook Grips

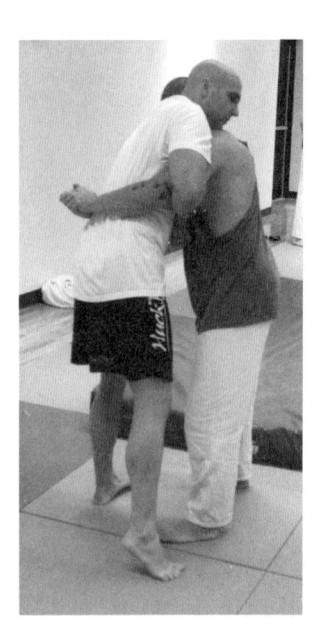

Kyle, on the right is doing a body lock on Alan. Anytime you grasp your hands together, locking your body to your opponent's body, this is a "body lock" and can be used in a variety of ways to throw or take your opponent down. By locking your hands together and pulling your opponent in to your hips, you are effectively breaking his posture and balance and setting him up for a throw or takedown. Alan, on the left, is using his arms to hook over Kyle's and will use them as a handle to throw or take Kyle down. This is a useful tie up for a variety of throws and takedowns.

High Collar Grip (1)

Ken is using his right hand to control Scott with a high collar grip. Don't make the mistake of inserting your right thumb into your opponent's collar. If you do, you trap your thumb and limit your movement quite a bit. Instead, grip as you see Ken is doing by gripping the collar or high on the jacket with your thumb out. You need to move your thumb freely to control your opponent. Notice that Ken is using his left hand to control Scott's sleeve above Scott's right elbow at about the triceps area.

High Collar Grip (2)

You can see how Ken is using his right hand and arm to control Scott as he attacks with his throw. If Ken had inserted his right thumb in Scott's collar, he wouldn't have the freedom of movement to better control his opponent.

Floating Elbow

Roy, on the left, has attacked Derrick with a forward throw where he has his right hand caught in Derrick's collar. This weakens his right hand (his steering hand) and in many situations, makes it useless. It's better to use your right hand (in this case) to wrap around your opponent's neck or use a back or loop grip to help control your opponent's body. The cause of a floating elbow is often when you have you have a high collar grip and hook your thumb in your opponent's collar, thus trapping it.

THE DIFFERENCE BETWEEN A THROW AND A TAKEDOWN

Throws

The primary function of a throw is to throw an opponent hard onto the mat or floor with control and force. In other words, your goal is to throw your opponent to the mat in such a way that groundfighting may not be necessary. Throw him with control and throw him hard. If you throw your opponent so hard that you take the starch out of him, it will soften him up for a good ground move, but more important, it could end the fight or match. It's advisable to follow-through to the mat after a throw to ensure victory and further control of your opponent, but in many cases, a good throw can end the fight, match or encounter right then and there.

Takedowns

The primary function of a takedown is to take an opponent to the mat or ground and finish him with a submission or other technique. Consider a takedown as a means of getting an opponent down to put him in a position so you can immediately follow-through with a finishing hold, submission technique or striking technique. The primary focus in a takedown is to get your opponent down to beat him once you've taken him down.

EFFECTIVE USE OF POSTURE, STANCE AND HIP DISTANCE

"Lead with your hips" is the best advice that can be given when talking about posture and position when engaged in standing situations. If you have your hips in good position to attack and defend with, you will be better able to control your opponent, the grip and how you throw him or defend against this throw. Often, the posture of your opponent (and you) dictates the type of grip you will use, which often dictates the particular attack you will choose to throw him with. As discussed in the Body Distances section, how close or far your hips are in relation to your opponent's hips dictates the action of the throw. Where (and how) you stand in relation to your opponent or in relation to the mat or surrounding area is important.

Your stance is important. How and where you stand in relation to your opponent often dictates what throw or takedown you will use (along with your grip and distance between your bodies). There are several stances used in judo, sambo, wrestling and other combat sports that bear study here.

In terms of posture, never allow your upper body to extend out in front of your hips (and your center of gravity) too far. If you lean forward too much, you are off-balance and your opponent can take advantage of this. If you always try to lower your body with your legs and not bend forward, you'll often have a good alignment in your stance.

Posture and Stance in the Initial Grip or Tie-up and Opposite Lead Legs

Chris, on the left, has a strong stance and has managed to pull Bob's shoulders forward and out in front of Bob's hips and center of balance. Chris is making sure to keep his knees flexed with his back relatively upright so his shoulders aren't out in front of his center of gravity. Chris also has his left foot as his sugar (lead) foot and makes sure to keep it outside of Bob's lead right foot. Chris has his left lead foot where it is so he can work to the outside (to Chris's left and Bob's right); duck under Bob's right extended arm and go for a Russian 2-on-1 tie up. Bob is leading with his right foot and wants to keep it inside of Chris's lead left foot. Often, a grappler who wants to use a right-sided throw will lead with his right leg or foot. If you are a left-side thrower, you may often lead with your left foot. This is true for this photo, as Chris prefers to throw to his left side and Bob prefers to throw to his right side. This is a common situation and the better grappler at body movement and grip fighting will prevail in controlling his opponent, and then be better able to throw him or take him down.

Core Skills

Lead With Your Hips

As Harry Parker used to say, "Lead with your hips." Ken, on the right, is leading with his right hip rather than stepping in with his right foot. If he would extend his right foot too far, he would leave himself open for a counter foot sweep throw from Scott. Also, leading with your hips gives you a better posture to attack and defend from, thus increasing your mobility. By leading with your hips, you are far better balanced and able to attack and defend. I always tell my athletes to try to keep their lead hip (if you're a right sided fighter, you will usually lead with your right hip) inside their opponent's lead hip. This way, you can move more easily either inside his hip or outside his hip, depending on the situation.

Your Sugar Foot Inside Opponent's Stance

You will usually lead with one foot or stand "square' when facing your opponent and fighting him. When you lead with one foot, this is what many people (including me) call the "sugar foot." Generally, if you are a right-handed thrower, you will lead with your right foot/leg. If you are a left-handed thrower, you will usually lead with your left foot/leg. Important aspects of your stance are that you never cross your legs unless you have a very good reason for it and make sure your feet and legs are normally directly underneath your hips so you can move freely and attack or defend quickly.

Your Sugar Foot Outside Opponent's Stance

Alan, on the right, has his right lead foot slightly to the outside and behind Chuck. He does this so he can shoot behind Chuck for a takedown or throw.

Your Sugar Foot in the Middle of Your Opponent's Square Stance

Bryan, on the right, has his right foot (his sugar foot) between Drew's feet. Bryan can use this lead foot to penetrate for an inner leg hook or use it to spin around for a forward throw.

Opposite Lead Legs

This photo shows how Chris, left, is leading with his left foot and Bob is leading with his right. Remember, it's most likely that you will throw off the same side you lead with. In this case, Chris is leading with his left foot and he will most likely use left-sided throws. Bob's sugar foot is his right foot and he most likely will attack with his right side. In cases like this, the athlete who imposes his will on his opponent and gets the better position using his grip and movement, will often get his attack in first (and most effectively).

Square Stance

John, at left, has squared his stance against Eric and makes sure to keep Eric from getting his left (sugar) foot and leg too much to the middle of John's stance. Some grapplers like to work out of a square stance. Those who do use the square stance have the ability to work to the inside or outside their opponents. Also notice how John is using the near shoulder tie up to control Eric. John is using his right hand and arm to pull down on Eric's left shoulder. This not only controls Eric's upper body, but also forces Eric to place a good amount of his body weight on his lead (left) foot, thus taking away some of his mobility. John also wants to pull Eric's upper body and shoulders forward so they are out in front of his hips. Doing this upsets Eric's balance and makes him vulnerable to a throw or takedown.

Square Stance (Low or Defensive Posture)

These two grapplers are very wary of each other and have their hips far apart to avoid contact and keep each other from scoring a throw or takedown. When both athletes are crouched over in this way, the tempo of the match is slow and defensive. Both athletes are off balance, and as a result, have to keep a wide stance to remain balanced. This isn't always a good position to be in, as you can't attack or defend freely from this bent-over, crouched posture.

Hips Far Apart (Fast Tempo)

Josh and Nikolay are wary of each other and as a result, each is keeping his hips leaning away from his opponent. This is a defensive posture, but as you can see, neither grappler is crouched over. A posture like this usually indicates a fast tempo for the match and there's a free exchange of attacks and defensive moves on the part of both athletes.

PHYSICAL FITNESS FOR THROWING

To perform a throw against a resisting, skilled, motivated and fit opponent, you should be physically able to do it. Physical fitness is necessary to perform and ultimately master a throwing skill. A major aspect of effective throws and takedowns is that you are physically fit enough to defend yourself and perform the skills necessary to defend yourself. Being physically able to perform a technique is an important part of the skill. Skill is the practical application of technique and to be able to apply a technique practically (with skill), fitness is vital. Remember what was said earlier about the ballistic movement of a throw and comparing it to a gun. If you're physically strong and have developed explosive power in the gym, you have a better chance of excelling in any athletic activity, especially throwing someone.

A GOOD DEFENSE CAN WIN FIGHTS

Probably one of the most neglected aspects of training in any for of sport combat is in the area of defense against throws or takedowns. While this book's focus isn't specifically on defense, it's safe to say that having a good defense can, and will, win matches for you. Really, defensive skills are integral to any grappling sport. As my good friend John Saylor has often said; "A good part of winning is not getting beat." What he means is that if you can defend yourself and stay competitive, there's always the possibility of gaining the advantage or beating your opponent.

Defensive skills are best when practiced on a regular basis. You can drill on these skills fairly often, if not every workout, and make sure when you are doing randori or going live with training partners, you actively put yourself in situations where you have to use your defense.

There are several "lines" of defense. **Grip fighting or pummeling** is the initial method of keeping an opponent at bay. Both offensive and defensive gripping skills are used to put an opponent into position so he can't attack effectively. In very real terms, using gripping as a means of defense is actually "preventative" defense. In other words, shutting your opponent down as much as possible with good grip fighting so that he can't launch an attack against you. Just as in medicine, an ounce of prevention is worth a pound of cure.

The second line of defense is **body movement**. This includes your use of body space; how close or far you are from your opponent. Making sure that you are in a position so your opponent can't effectively attack by your use of posture, grip or how fast you move about the mat. When speaking about body movement, your posture is very much part of it all. A bent-over body with poor weight distribution is much easier to throw than a body that's well balanced.

The third line of defense is really an extension of good posture and movement. **Using the hips to block an attack** is probably the most effective method of stopping a throw. For instance, in the hip block, the defender will use his left hip to block, or jam, his opponent's right sided throwing attack. The defender won't allow the attacker to get past his left hip. From this, the defender stops the momentum of the forward throwing attack and regains his balance to re-establish himself as a threat to his opponent. Basically, you cut with your opposite hip, hit him hard with that hip and don't let your opponent get past your hip. If he slips his hip in, he can still catch you in a throw, so block his attack hard. The defender should also "cut away" from the attack if possible. As you block with your left hip, tear your right hand away from his grasp and maybe even step back a bit with your right leg and foot. Really cut hard and it will stop his forward momentum.

The fourth line of defense is to **hop around** your opponent's attack. I don't prefer this movement as your basic defensive skill, but it does work. However, it can also get you in trouble. When at attacker comes in for a right forward throw, the defender will literally hop around the throw to his right. This works some of the time, but if the attacker is really dedicated to the attack, he will fit in a second time as the defender finishes his hopping evasive action. The attacker will do what is called a "double take." That is, he will hit in immediately with the same throw as soon as the defender hops around. One time, at the Pan American Judo Championships, I watched a guy hop around his opponent's shoulder throw and the second he hopped, the attacker followed up with a second shoulder throw and buried him into the mat. The best method of defense in hopping around is to hop around the attack and try to make as much distance or space between you and the attacker. As you hop around, try to crouch over and make a lot of space between your hips and the attacker's hips and body, and make sure you don't lean on the attacker as you hop around him. He will catch you if you do.

The fifth line of defense is to **lower you body below his center of gravity and sag**. You will often do this in combination with a hip block, but not always. When doing this line of defense along with a hip block, you set your opponent up for a great counter throw with a Buck or other rear-lifting throw.

The sixth line of defense is to **cut against the grain of the throw**. When your opponent attacks you with a forward throw, you cut against the direction, flow or "grain" of the throw. This movement stops his momentum and throws him off balance and gives you an opportunity to counter him with a throw or takedown of your own.

The seventh line of defense is a **sprawl** against a front double leg takedown or other move where your opponent shoots a takedown at you. Work hard on not only your sprawl technique, but also hitting him hard with your hips as you sprawl back aggressively. Don't be happy to only survive his shoot, but try to smash his face into the mat as you sprawl.

The eighth line of defense is to **jam your leg between his** when he tries a lifting or pick up throw on you. Jamming your leg between the thrower's legs stops the upward movement in his lift and buys you some time.

The ninth line of defense is to **evade** the throw. The Japanese call this "sukashi" which means to evade. As your opponent attacks with an Inner Thigh throw, for example, you side step his attack and can counter by using your hands to turn him over forward.

The last line of defense is to **turn out of the throw** and is a last-ditch attempt at avoiding being thrown onto your back. This is the least recommended line of defense and should be done only by skilled, elite athletes who have excellent kinesthetic awareness. Turning out is when the attacker has actually thrown you and you have to twist your body enough to land on your front or front side so that a minimal score is awarded.

Under no circumstances should you ever, and I mean ever, land in a bridge position when thrown on your back or taken down. Landing in a bridge position to avoid landing on your back is extremely dangerous and you could break your neck or suffer other serious injuries.

Here are a few examples of the lines of defense discussed. These are basic examples and each athlete in each and every situation is different, but if you have a good awareness of how important defense is, it can literally win matches for you.

Hip Block and Cut Away

Bryan is defending against Drew's forward throw by using a hip block. Drew has attacked Bryan with a left-sided forward throw and Bryan has jammed his right hip hard against Drew's left hip, stopping Drew's forward momentum and stopping the throw.

Throws and Takedowns

Hop Around Defense

This first photo shows Kirk attacking Kevin with a shoulder throw and Kevin has created space between the two bodies by backing away a bit.

As Kevin backs away, he hops around to his right to avoid Kirk's attack. Kevin wants to create as much space between his body and Kirk's as possible to avoid Kirk's throw. You can see that Kirk is still a threat and can hit in with a "double take" and still possibly throw Kevin.

Lower Your Body and Sag

Roman has lowered his body below Nikolay's center of gravity and has stopped Nikolay's forward throw. Roman is in a good position to take Nikolay to the mat by simply continuing to squat and turn into Nikolay or Roman can use a Buck to throw him.

Leg Jam Defense Against Opponent's Lifting Throw

Josh has hooked his right leg inside of Derrick's left leg to stop the lifting action of Derrick's throw. This is often the best defense you can muster if your opponent has started to lift you and you are going up in the air off the mat! Josh can turn this into an inside leg hook counter or go for an Thigh Lift or Leg Wrap throw as well.

Cut Against the Grain of the Throw

Chuck has attacked Alan with a Head and Arm throw and Alan has cut against the direction or "grain" of the throw as his defense. You can see that this type of defense lends directly to an excellent counter throw for Alan. Alan has lowered the level of his body as he shifted against the direction of Chuck's attack. Doing this not only stopped the forward momentum of Chuck's attack, but it broke his balance as well. Alan then countered with his own throw.

Evade the Attack

Josh (on the right) has attacked with a forward throw and Kirk evades the throw by using his right leg to step out and away as he lifts his left leg to move around Josh. Kirk also turns his hips so that his left hip is leading as he evades the attack. Kirk can continue on and use the momentum of Josh's forward attack and counter with a forward throw of his own.

Sprawl Defense

Kirk has shot in for a double leg takedown or throw and Josh uses his hands and arms to snap Kirk down on the mat as he shoots his legs back wide (for better balance and stability). Josh makes sure to drive Kirk down face first onto the mat so that his forward momentum is stopped. Josh also drives his hips forward and to the mat as low as possible to stop Kirk's attack and keep Kirk from trying to get behind him. This is a common, but outstanding, defense against an opponent who shoots in for a double or single leg attack.

Throws and Takedowns

SECTION TWO:
Lifting Throws

"Your opponent should fear your first attack."
John Saylor

Throws and Takedowns

John Saylor's quote about your opponent fearing your first attack describes the psychological impact of Lifting throws. If you're known as someone who can lift an opponent up in the air and slam him down hard onto the mat, people will be less inclined to want to fight you. Whether a Lifting throw is your first attack or not isn't really the point; the fact that you can throw someone with resounding impact gives you the edge in most every fight. In much the same way a knockout artist in boxing can end a fight with one punch, a grappler who can throw with extreme control and force is feared.

These throws are any that you lift your opponent up and throw him to the mat. You'll lift him primarily with your hip(s), leg, knee, thigh or foot but sometimes with your hands, arms or other body part as well. Lifting throws differ from Pick Ups or Leg Grabs in that they more often than not rely on lifting your opponent with your lower body rather than with your upper body along with the explosive rotation of your body as you throw him.

Lifting throws work because of two dynamic factors: (1) the explosive rotation of the person's body doing the throw and (2) his use of a body part (leg, thigh, hip or other) to lift, sweep, prop or hook the opponent. What may look like brute strength in lifting an opponent off the mat to throw him is often the result of an initial explosive hip rotation and footwork followed immediately by a lifting action.

Knowing how to perform lifting throws is an important and fundamental technical skill in sambo. The innovators of lifting throws, the Japanese, used lifting throws primarily as counter throws and not usually as offensive weapons. Using lifting throws as aggressive, offensive throwing attacks was innovated by the Soviets through their development of sambo and when these throws were first seen in international competition as offensive throws, they changed the way the world looked at this type of throw. As with other sambo coaches, I introduce lifting throws early in an athlete's career. If viewed as an offensive move, rather than primarily as a counter move, lifting throws are an important part of a new athlete's arsenal of throws, and they only get better as the athlete matures and progresses in skill, fitness and technical awareness.

The Buck

This is an important throw and is known by various names, depending on your approach to grappling. In judo and many styles of jujitsu, it's known as Ura Nage (Rear Throw). In sambo, I've heard it called the Chair Throw since it looks like the thrower is sitting down in a chair. Somewhere along the line at Welcome Mat, we started to call this move the "Buck" simply because you bucked your opponent up and over your hip and flattened him hard on the mat. The name stuck. It was, and is, an easy name to remember and that's why it has this name for this book. This is an aggressive attack that has the capacity to slam your opponent hard onto the mat. The reason this is an important throw is because it's essential to learn how to lift and rotate your opponent when throwing him. This throw (and it's many variations) works so well in all forms of grappling and sport combat and can be used by anyone of any weight class, male and female. Many people think of it as a "power" throw, but that is completely wrong. This throw is a powerful body slam that works on the key elements of control and force. It's a dynamic throw that works because of the tremendous explosive and plyometric effect the throw has.

In this approach to the Buck, Derrick (on the left) moves to Josh's right side. Derrick quickly steps to the outside of Josh's right hip and leg as shown and uses his left hand to "tight waist" Josh around the hip. The term "tight waist" means that Derrick is reaching around Josh's hip, grabbing it and pulling it in tight for control. Derrick's head is an important part of this throw and Derrick has started to drive his head to the inside of Josh's right shoulder as shown.

Lifting Throws

Derrick has locked in his tight waist with his left hand and arm (grabbing Josh's left hip bone with his left hand) for good control of Josh's hips. Derrick has shot in with his left foot and his left front hip is wedged against Josh's right hip and buttocks. Derrick lowers his level using his legs and squats almost as if sitting in a chair. Derrick's head is wedged in tightly against the front of Josh's right shoulder and pectoral and has good control with his left hand on Josh's lapel. Derrick has effectively closed all body space between his body and Josh's body and is squatting low under Josh's hips, below Josh's center of gravity. Derrick's feet are wide apart and he is well balanced. Derrick is ready to lift Josh for the throw.

Derrick has driven hard off both feet and in an explosive manner started to lift Josh up and into the throw. Notice how Derrick is lifting Josh and has Josh riding on his left hip.

Throws and Takedowns

Derrick is driving hard with his legs and lower body and this plyometric effect is lifting Josh. Derrick is turning his head (still controlling Josh's left shoulder) to the left and into the direction of the throw.

The throw is in full effect and Josh is being lifted and rotated to his backside.

Lifting Throws

Derrick is starting to rotate strongly to his left and this action causes Josh to fall harder and faster to his backside. Your head is crucial in this throw as your body goes in the direction your head turns and Derrick's head is turning to his left, causing his body to rotate in that direction.

Derrick is rotating hard to his left and the combination of his lift and rotation causes Josh to be thrown.

Throws and Takedowns

Here's a back view of the lift and rotation of this throw. Notice how Derrick's head is turning to the left and into the direction of the throw. Derrick has a strong tight waist with his left hand and arm on Josh's hip.

Look at how Derrick's body rotates and drives Josh up and over into the throw.

Lifting Throws

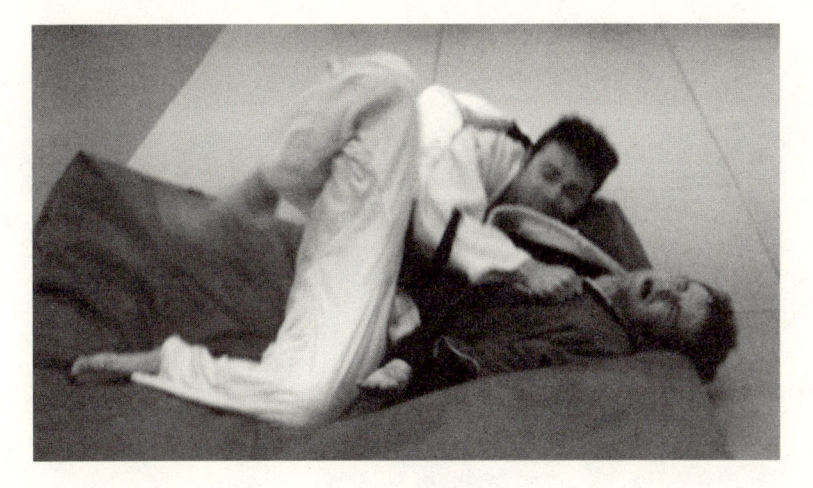

Derrick rotates over completely and lands on Josh as he finishes the throw. You can see why crash pads are necessary!

The action of lifting and rotating your opponent is a key element in throwing him. This photo shows Kolden exploding into a Buck with tremendous lift and rotation. Notice that Kolden has a tremendous back arch as well and this is an important element of this throw. However, the arch is the result of an explosive lift and rotation, along with a solid base with one or both feet firmly planted on the mat.

The Buck (No Jacket)

Alan, on the right, and Chuck are tied up. Alan makes it a point to have his right foot on the outside of Chuck's lead foot (his left).

Alan lowers his level of his body by bending his knees and steps behind Chuck with his right foot as shown. As he does this, Alan uses his left hand to pull in on Chuck's right elbow, trapping Chuck's right arm against his belly. Alan uses his right hand to reach around Chuck's back and tight waist Chuck.

Here's another view of how Alan has gone behind Chuck and tight waisted him.

Alan squats low as if he were sitting in a chair as he uses his right hand to pull Chuck in. Alan continues to use his left hand to drive Chuck's right elbow tighter into Chuck's belly. Alan is planted firmly on both of his feet.

Throws and Takedowns

Here's another view of how Alan squats low and is about to throw Chuck.

Here's a view of the throw caught in action. Alan is squatting low and below Chuck's hips and buttocks and under his center of gravity.

Lifting Throws

Alan throws Chuck and makes it a point to rotate onto Chuck (chest to chest) as he finishes the throw.

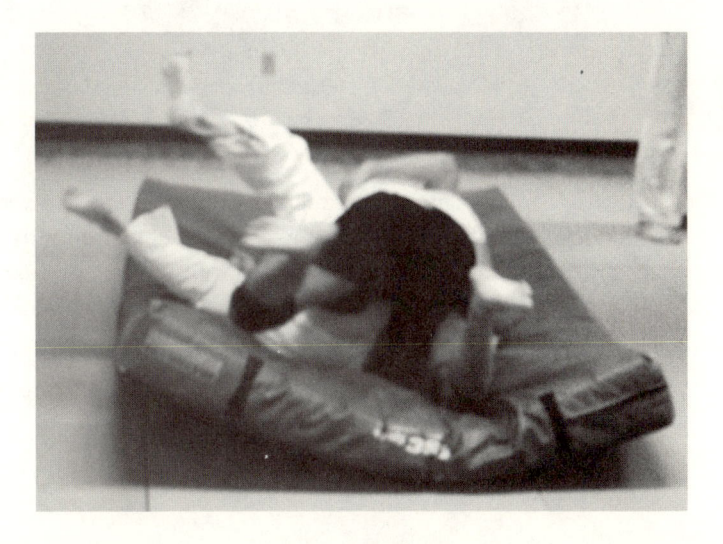

Alan finishes the throw landing hard on Chuck.

The Buck as a Counter to the Sweeping Hip Throw

One of the most common ways to first learn the Buck is as a counter to a forward throw. The Buck is often used as an effective counter to any forward throw or attack and it's especially useful as a counter to a Sweeping Hip or Inner Thigh throw.

In this photo, Roy (on the left) has attacked Derrick with a Sweeping Hip throw. Derrick immediately defends by using his left hip to hit Roy's right buttocks and hip. Derrick also uses his left hand to jam or push into Roy's back as shown in his initial defense of Roy's attack. As he does this, Derrick starts to squat and lower the level of his body as if he were sitting in a chair.

This photo shows how Derrick has tight waisted with his left arm around Roy's hips and lowered his level by squatting below Roy's buttocks and hips. By lowering his body level this way, Derrick has gone under Roy's center of gravity and broken his balance. Also notice that Roy's right arm is bent with the elbow sticking up in the air. This is what is called a "floating elbow" and doesn't usually give the attacker (in this case, Roy) very much control of his opponent. Derrick has pretty much nullified Roy's right arm by using his left arm to control Roy's waist and crowding Roy's right arm completely, making it useless. Derrick has a strong base with his legs and is about to explode into the throw.

Derrick is lifting Roy and beginning to elevate him. As Derrick lifts, he also rotates his body to his left (into Roy) and this action, along with the explosive lift is what creates the momentum and speed that will multiply the force of the throw. Notice that Derrick's head isn't tucked in Roy's right shoulder and pectoral area which would normally give Derrick more control of Roy's body. The reason Derrick's head is further away from Roy's shoulder is the initial position of Roy's right arm. Had Roy used his right arm to reach around Derrick's head, it would have enabled Derrick to use his head as another tool to control and throw Roy. When your opponent has his right elbow floating in the way Roy does, there is a bit less control that the thrower (Derrick) has in his counter, but Derrick's tight waist and control of Roy's hips and upper body is sufficient for a good throw anyway.

Lifting Throws

This photo shows how Derrick is using his head on the front of Josh's shoulder (high on the pectoral) to control Josh better in the throw. Josh is attacking with a forward throw with his right arm around Derrick's neck (and not with a floating elbow). Remember, your body goes in the direction of your head so it's vital for Derrick to turn his head in the direction of the throw.

Derrick is completing the throw and turning his body to his left explosively so that he lands on Roy as he finishes the throw. Notice Derrick's head is turning to the left (in the direction of Roy and the throw) and his feet are driving hard off the mat and his knees driving into the throw creating a good back arch. This is a hard throw and one of the most effective counters to any forward throw your opponent may use.

Buck Counter to Opponent's Leg Jam

The best way to stop your opponent from bucking you and picking you up is to hook your leg onto his leg. Doing this keeps him from lifting you. Derrick is behind Josh and is starting to lift him for the Buck.

Here's a back view of how Josh has jammed his right leg in and hooked it around Derrick's leg to keep Derrick from lifting him. Josh will try to turn into Derrick and throw him onto his back with an Inner Leg Hook as the counter to the initial attack that Derrick made.

Lifting Throws

Here's the front view of how Josh has jammed his leg in and hooked it around Derrick's leg to defend against the pick up. To counter Josh's leg jam and avoid being thrown flat onto his back, Derrick lowers the level of his body by squatting.

Derrick hops around to his right as he uses his left hand and arm to grab around Josh's far hip and tight waist him. Derrick's head is low and moving along with his right leg as he hops.

Throws and Takedowns

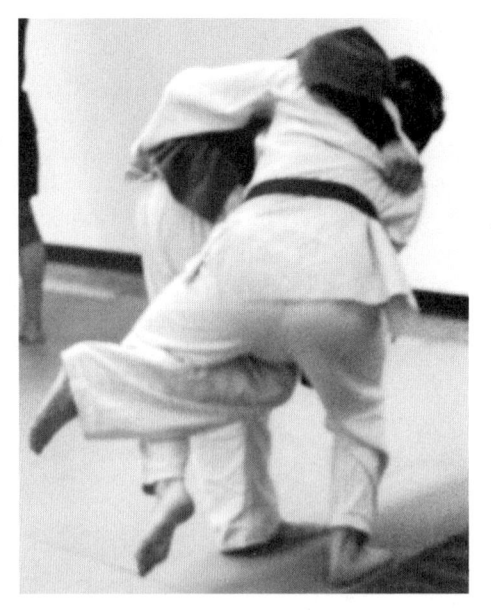

Derrick continues to hop around Josh and pull him closer to his body setting him up for the throw.

Derrick has moved around Josh at about 180 degrees and plants his right foot firmly on the mat as he uses his left hand to control Josh's waist. Derrick has used his right hand to continue to grab Josh's left lapel through the entire sequence.

Lifting Throws

Derrick uses the momentum of his body hopping around Josh to throw him with the Buck.

Derrick finishes the throw by landing chest to chest on Josh to get maximum points for the throw.

Throws and Takedowns

The Buck Outside Thigh Sweep (Lift)

Alan and Chuck are tied up with Alan's right foot to the outside of Chuck's left (lead) foot.

Alan moves his body behind Chuck as shown, using his left hand to drive Chuck's right elbow to his belly. Alan uses his right arm to tight waist Chuck at the far (right) hip

Lifting Throws

As Alan uses his right arm to control Chuck's right hip, Alan moves his body to his right. This movement drives Chuck's body to Chuck's right side.

Alan continues to move as far as he can to his right and has Chuck firmly tight waisted. Alan is about to use his right foot and leg to hook Chuck's right leg and throw him.

Alan hooks Chuck with his right leg as shown as he drives hard to his right. Alan is driving hard off his left foot.

You can see how Alan has kept his head firmly planted on Chuck's left shoulder and not ducked under. Ducking under will lessen the control and force of the throw. Notice how Alan's right foot is hooked around the outside of Chucks' right lower leg as he throws him.

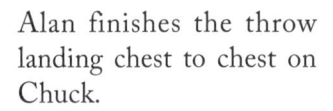

Alan finishes the throw landing chest to chest on Chuck.

Inside Thigh Lift
(also called Leg Wrap or Leg Lace Throw)

As with some other throws in this book, this throw has been referred to as the "Kharbarelli" in international judo. Named after Olympic Champion Shota Kharbarelli, this throw is an explosive, dynamic lifting throw still considered unorthodox in the sport of judo.

Nikolay, on the left, has used his right foot and leg to entwine around the inside of Derrick's left leg as shown. Notice how Nikolay's right foot is hooked onto Derrick's left lower leg. Nikolay is using his right arm and hand to control Derrick with a strong back grip. Nikolay's left hand is holding onto Derrick's right lapel (not shown).

Nikolay uses his left foot to step around to the front of Derrick's body, creating a strong rotation in Nikolay's body. As he does this, Nikolay uses his right arm to pull Derrick's body in closer to his.

Here's another view of how Nikolay has stepped around into the front of Derrick with his left foot. You can see the start of the rotation of Nikolay's body as he does this. Notice that Nikolay's head is starting to turn to his right, adding more power to the throwing attack.

As Nikolay uses his left foot to step deep, he turns his body with his hips to his right in an explosive motion. Notice that Nikolay still has good control with his right foot locked onto Derrick's left lower leg. This photo shows Nikolay's body starting to turn into the direction of the throw.

Lifting Throws

As Nikolay explosively turns his body, he continues to pull with his right hand on Derrick's back. Nikolay lifts his right leg between Derrick's legs as shown, causing Derrick to be lifted into the air. The combination of Nikolay's explosive body rotation and the lifting action of his right leg, along with using his right hand to lock Derrick's body to his body, enable Nikolay to throw Derrick.

Here is the throw at the peak of its movement. Nikolay continues to turn his body to his right as he throws Derrick.

Throws and Takedowns

Here's another view of the throw at the peak of its effort.

Nikolay finishes the throw by landing on Derrick with maximum force and control.

Inner Thigh Throw to Low Inside Thigh Lift (Leg Lace) Throw Combination

In this approach to the Leg Wrap (or Leg Lace) throw, Josh attacks Derrick with an Uchi Mata (Inner Thigh Throw) initially. Whether Josh really intends to use Uchi Mata to throw Derrick, or if he uses it to fake Derrick out isn't important. The important thing is that Josh is using his Uchi Mata to sink his right leg in between Derrick's legs so he can throw him.

For any number of reasons, Josh senses that his Inner Thigh throw won't work. Often, Derrick has lowered his body and started a good defense. As a result, Josh uses his left shoulder to roll or drive into Derrick, and as he does this, Josh ducks his head forward. This created momentum for Josh toward Derrick's right shoulder.

Throws and Takedowns

Josh continues to roll his left shoulder and head forward into Derrick as he uses his left foot to hop around and inside Derrick's stance (close to Derrick's right foot). This rolling and stepping action is circular in nature and causes Josh to lower his body level. As Josh does this, he uses his left hand (holding Derrick's right sleeve) to drive Derrick's right arm into his belly for control. Notice that Josh has used his right foot to lock onto the inside of Derrick's left lower leg, controlling it.

Josh continues his roll into Derrick and he uses his right hand to pull Derrick into the throwing action.

Lifting Throws

Here's another view of how Josh has explosively rolled into Derrick and he sits under him and about to throw him.

Here is the throw in the middle of the action. Notice how Josh is using his right hand to pull Derrick into the direction of the throw.

Josh continues to roll Derrick into the throw and will finish by rolling over on top of him.

Front Thigh Lift from a Looping Grip and Inside Leg Hook Attack

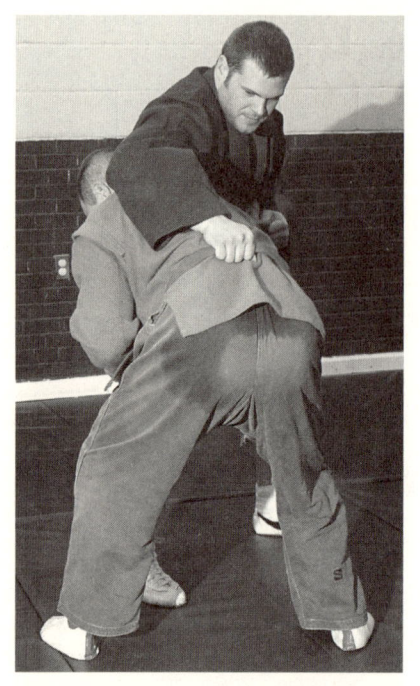

This is similar to the Leg Wrap (Lace) throw because it relies on the attacker's base leg to step into his opponent as he rotates his opponent with his (the attacker's) hip and body movement. Here's another variation of the Kharbarelli Pick Up, as it's called in sport judo. This time, however, the attacker, Trevor, is attempting to throw Bryan with an Inside Leg Hook, either as a real attempt to throw, or as a fake to sucker Bryan into the Front Thigh Lift.

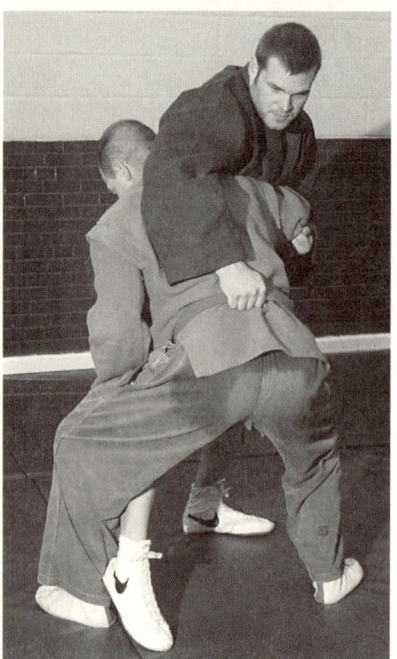

Trevor is using his right leg and foot to attack Bryan with a Major Inner Hook. Trevor is using his right hand to grab Bryan's belt in a looping grip. Trevor also is using his left hand to grab Bryan's right elbow.

If Trevor senses it, he can throw Bryan with a Major Inner Hook from this position by simply driving into Bryan, using his right leg to hook Bryan's left leg (as shown) and drive him onto his back. However, Bryan may have shifted his weight forward and used his left leg to hook Trevor's right leg as a counter throw. In this case, Trevor will use his left foot to step forward deeply to start his Thigh Lift. Notice that in this attack, Trevor has used his left hand to grab Bryan's pant leg immediately above the knee. This extra handle will help lift Bryan into the throw.

Throws and Takedowns

Trevor has stepped in forward with his left foot deeply between Bryan's legs. As Trevor does this, he quickly starts to rotate his body to his left as he uses his right hand to lift Bryan holding the belt as a good handle and his right elbow to push down hard on Bryan's upper back and shoulders to "steer" Bryan's upper body into the direction of the throw. Trevor is using his left hand to lift Bryan's leg by the pant leg. As he does this, Trevor explosively lifts with his base leg (his left leg) as he uses his right leg to lift Bryan's body. Trevor's right leg is slightly bent and still is hooking Bryan's left leg as shown to assist in the lifting action. This explosive rotation and lifting action happening all at once is the action that makes the throw work.

Lifting Throws

Here's another view of the lifting and rotating action that Trevor is using to throw Bryan. Look at how Trevor's right elbow is driving hard into Bryan's upper back as Trevor uses his right hand on the belt to continue in the lifting and pulling action.

Trevor drives Bryan over with the throw and rotates into him causing Bryan to land flat onto his back as shown. You can see how Trevor has used his legs to drive off the mat for maximum effect.

Throws and Takedowns

Outer Thigh Sweep Throw

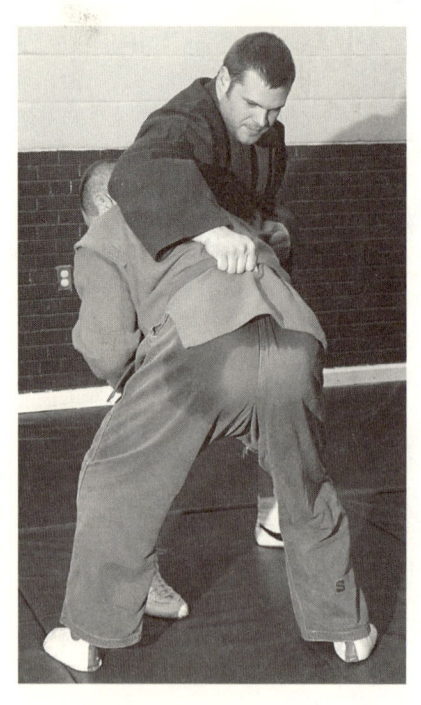

Trevor has broken Bryan's posture with a looping grip using his right hand on Bryan's belt.

Trevor uses his left foot to step forward as he steps back to his right rear with his right foot. As he does this, Trevor uses his right elbow and arm to pull in and down on Bryan forcing Bryan to lean to his left front corner as shown. Trevor turns to his right side as he steps back and uses his left hand to push Bryan in the direction of the throw. This action forces Bryan to his left front corner and off balance.

Lifting Throws

As Bryan leans to his front left corner, Trevor rotates explosively to his right as he continues to use his right hand to steer Bryan in the direction of the throw. Trevor quickly uses his right leg as shown in the bent position to sweep Bryan's left upper leg. Trevor sweeps inward with his right thigh as shown as he pulls Bryan forward toward Bryan's left front corner. This explosive rotation and sweeping action with the thigh causes Bryan to be thrown.

Foot Prop Throw from a Looping Grip

This throw is a variation of the Outer Thigh Sweep and uses the weight of the thrower's body and the sudden block of his foot to make the throw work. This also shows how powerful the looping grip is and how you can use your (in this case) right elbow and arm to steer your opponent over into a throw. This throw is ideal for opponents who fight from a low, crouched stance or are defensive and have their shoulders and upper body too far forward in front of their hips.

Jarrod has a strong looping grip on Eric who is in a low posture. To break Eric's posture and balance more, Jarrod will use his right elbow and arm to drive down on Eric's upper back. This forces Eric to lean forward more and puts him off balance forward. Jarrod makes it a point to place his left foot close and to the front of Eric's right foot as shown.

Jarrod uses his right elbow to drive down on Eric's upper back forcing him to lean forward toward Eric's left shoulder. As he does this, Jarrod stays planted on his left foot and quickly lowers his body by bending his knees. Jarrod uses his left hand and arm to push into Eric a bit and lock him in place. This throw differs from the Kodokan Judo version of this throw in a few distinct ways. (1) The attacker lowers the level of his body below his opponent's center of gravity. (2) The attacker's initial grip forces his opponent's body to bend forward and into the direction of the throw. (3) The attacker often uses the explosive rotation of his own body to whip his opponent over as he blocks or props his foot. In the judo version (which works very well also), the attacker lifts and pulls the defender as he props or blocks his foot. This sambo approach was developed for opponents who fight from a low, crouched position often seen in sambo.

This shows Jarrod continue to lower his body level and use his right foot to block or prop Eric's left foot at the front of his ankle. As Jarrod does this, he quickly rotates his hips to the right rear corner. As Jarrod rotates to his right, he continues to use his right elbow and arm to drive Eric forward over his left shoulder into the direction of the throw.

The action of Jarrod quickly lowering his level below Eric's center of gravity and his explosive rotation into the direction of the throw (in this case, to Jarrod's right) cause Eric to fall forward over his left shoulder. Jarrod's lowering of his body below Eric's center of gravity and his quick rotation to his right are the actions that create the momentum to throw Eric. Jarrod could also use his left foot to step forward if he wished, to add to the rotation of the throw. Jarrod uses his right foot to block or prop Eric's left foot at the front of Eric's ankle. Doing this isolates Eric's left foot and leg and forces Eric's upper body to be thrown at a greater rate of speed forward and over his left shoulder.

Lifting Throws

Here's a back view of how Jarrod uses his right foot to block or prop Eric's left foot and front ankle. It's important for Jarrod to continue to use his right elbow and arm to steer Eric into the direction of the throw. Jarrod's right forearm is firmly on Eric's back and Jarrod's right hand is firmly grabbing Eric's belt.

Jarrod continues to rotate to this right and finishes the throw by completely whipping his body over and landing on Eric. This follow through action is necessary to get the full effect of the throw.

Thigh Sweep Throw

This throw is similar to the Sliding Foot Sweep, and in fact, has many traits similar to that throw. This is throw that proves that good timing is important to throwing an opponent.

Ken, on the left, is facing Scott and Ken makes sure that he is about a half step or step to his right in relation to Scott's body. You can see Ken's right foot about a step to the left of Scott in this photo. This is important so Ken has room to sweep his right leg fully when he attacks Scott with the throw. Notice that Ken's right hand shoulder grip is trapping and controlling Scott's left side. Ken's left hand is gripping Scott's right lapel.

Ken moves Scott to Ken's left (and Scott's right) in a rapid movement. "The faster you go, the easier you throw" is a bit of bad poetry I use to teach this movement. But it's true; the faster Ken moves Scott, the more momentum he creates to throw Scott.

Lifting Throws

See how Ken is a full step behind Scott as he has moved Scott to Ken's left and Scott's right. As Scott brings his feet together (as shown) Ken will use his right thigh to attack Scott.

As Ken forces Scott to move, Ken uses his right knee and thigh to sweep Scott at Scott's left upper leg. Ken is moving rapidly as he does this, relying on the fast tempo and speed of the bodies to make the throw work.

Throws and Takedowns

Ken sweeps Scott using his right thigh and knee as shown. Notice that Ken's right knee is making contact on Scott's left upper thigh and buttocks and has driven Scott's legs and feet close together. It is essential for Ken to use the movement of the bodies and not try to lift Scott with his hands. Ken's hands merely lock him to Scott and he doesn't use them to pull or lift Scott in any way.

Ken is sweeping Scott and throwing him. You can see how Ken is sweeping with is right thigh.

Ken finishes the throw by holding onto Scott with both hands, making sure he controls Scott's body all the way to the mat and lands him flat on his back.

Belly-to-Belly Throw

This throw is seen often in Olympic wrestling and is ideal for any type of sport combat. Roman is locking his hands together around Josh, making sure he has trapped the right arm of Josh with his left arm and elbow as shown. Roman moves his body as close as possible to Josh and actually tries to get his belly to touch Josh's belly. By doing this, Roman has not only locked his body onto Josh to throw him, but completely controls Josh's movement. Roman lowers the level of his body and squats enough so that his hips are lower than Josh's hips. Getting below Josh's center of gravity is important in making this throw work.

Roman quickly uses his right foot to step forward and as he does, drives his right hip hard into Josh's left hip. As he does this simultaneous step and explosive lift, Roman explosively arches his body to his left rear. Notice how Roman has used his left arm to trap Josh's right arm to prevent Josh from using his left arm to try to stop the throw or catch himself.

Lifting Throws

Roman keeps his belly locked onto Josh's belly and turns into the direction of the throw as he throws Josh over.

Roman finishes the throw by landing on Josh, still locked onto him and belly-to-belly. This is a hard throw, so make sure you practice it on crash pads! Remember, you can adapt this throw in any number of ways, using the jacket or in "no gi" situations.

Throws and Takedowns

SECTION THREE:
Pick Ups and Leg Grabs

"Kuzushi is the description for the 'sum total' of movement. One's entire body through grip, posture, and body space, opponent's reaction and movement (ballistic and momentum) all create the 'perfect storm.'"

Jim Bregman

Throws and Takedowns

Pick Ups and Leg Grabs can be both spectacular and subtle. Spectacular when you pick your opponent up off the mat and slam him back down for a loud thud. Subtle when you pick or grab your opponent's ankle and take him to the mat, setting him up for a submission technique or pin. Some people consider these moves as simply a way to get your opponent to the mat to finish him, but these throws have power as well.

The common trait among Pick Ups and Leg Grabs is the thrower's use of his upper body (hands, arms, shoulders and sometimes the hips) to throw or take his opponent to the mat. Basically, if you grab, scoop or manipulate your opponent using your hands and arms and throw him, it's often referred to as a Pick Up or Leg Grab.

In some cases, these types of throws are the "bread and butter" moves for a grappler. In other cases, these throws and takedowns happen as the result of linking moves together or in the flurry of the action. Knowing how to grab your opponent's leg or legs from a variety of angles and situations is important in having a complete arsenal of throws and takedowns.

Cuban Leg Grab (No Jacket)

The Cuban Leg Grab is basically a single leg throw that packs an extra wallop. Alan is leading with his right foot to the outside of Chuck's stance and slightly behind Chuck's left foot. Alan has a near shoulder underhook and arm tie up to start.

Alan bends his knees to lower the level of his body and uses his left hand and arm to grab the inside of Chuck's left leg immediately above the knee.

Pick Ups and Leg Grabs

Here's another view of how Alan lowers the level of his body and uses his left hand to grab inside and immediately above Chuck's left knee. Alan is using his right hand and arm to tightwaist Chuck and control his hips.

Alan drives forward, using his left hand to scoop or pick up Chuck's left leg. Alan can "run" with the throw and increase the velocity by taking a few steps in the direction of the throw. Alan makes it a point to lift Chuck's leg up high and to Alan's left hip, making the throw that much harder. Alan uses his head as a wedge to jam in the front left shoulder or pectoral area of Chuck as he throws him. This controls Chuck's upper body well.

Cuban Leg Grab (Using Jacket)

Here is the version of the Cuban Leg Grab using the jacket. I gave this move its name because when I was in Cuba, the athletes from that country used this throw with excellent results.

Chris, on the right, is using his left hand to grab Derrick's right shoulder.

Chris drops in low, lowering the level of his body by bending his knees. As he does this, Chris controls Derrick's body by using his left elbow to drive down (elbow straight down as shown in the photo). This helps break Derrick's balance. Chris also uses his head to drive into Derrick's right shoulder and pectoral area. As he does this, Chris reaches in with his right hand to grab Derrick's right leg.

Pick Ups and Leg Grabs

Here's another view of how Chris drops in low and starts his attack with this throw. Notice how Chris is using his right hand to grab Derrick's right leg immediately above the knee. You can see how Chris is driving into Derrick by how Chris has his right foot planted on the mat and his body is driving into Derrick.

Chris uses his right hand to pick up Derrick's right leg as shown. Look at how Chris is using his left hand grabbing the jacket and how his left elbow is driving straight down to the mat to disrupt Derrick's balance.

Chris is driving into the throw. Chris makes it a point to lift Derrick's right leg to Chris' right hip (or higher) to get as much elevation into the throw as possible.

Chris is driving into the throw and throwing Derrick. This is a hard throw and flattens your opponent.

Other Places to Grab

Scooping your right hand through the middle of your opponent's legs up and into his crotch is another way of grabbing his lower body. Drive your hand right up through is crotch with as much force as you wish. Driving your hand and arm up through his crotch softens him up and allows you to scoop really hard producing a harder throw.

You can also use your grabbing hand (in this case, Derrick's right hand and arm) and use it to scoop your opponent's far (in this case, Chris's left) leg immediately above his knee. Notice how Derrick has turned his hand so that it's palm up. This gives you better control of his leg when grabbing or scooping it.

The Metz

Ken is using a Russian 2 on 1 grip and is using his left hand to grab low on Scott's left sleeve and his right hand to hook into Scott's left armpit area. He is bending over to slow the action and break Scott's balance forward.

Here's another view of how Ken uses a 2 on 1 grip to control Scott.

Ken starts to move to his right and to the left, outside Scott's stance as shown. Ken starts to uses his right hand to grab between Scott's legs.

Ken has his right foot to the rear, behind Scott's left leg and is using his left hand to pull Scott's left arm to Ken's chest. As he does this, Ken is using his right hand to reach through Scott's legs.

Throws and Takedowns

Ken drives into Scott with his right shoulder and as he does, he uses his right hand to reach and hook his hand behind Scott's right knee.

Ken uses his right hand to hook behind Scott's right knee as he drives into Scott.

Pick Ups and Leg Grabs

Here's another view of how Ken uses his right hand to grab Scott's right leg. Notice how Ken is squatting low and under Scott's buttocks and center of gravity.

Ken uses his right hand to grab and scoop behind Scott's right knee and as he does, drive hard into Scott, throwing him.

To get extra power into the throw, Ken uses his right arm to hook and lift up on Scott's right leg at the knee. Ken drives to his right rear shoulder as he throws Scott.

Ken drives Scott to the mat flat on his back to finish the throw.

Front Double Leg with Thigh Lift

Kolden drops low and shoots in for a Double Leg on Derrick. Kolden is leading with his right leg as he attacks.

Kolden places his head on Derrick's right hip as he scoops with both hands on Derrick's legs.

As Kolden lifts Derrick with both of his hands and arms, he uses his head to drive up and to his right (and into Derrick's right ribcage). Doing this drives Derrick to his left. As he does this, Kolden uses his right legs and knee to sweep and lift Derrick's left leg immediately above the knee. This entire action drives Derrick to his left side and to Kolden's right side.

Kolden continues to scoop and lift with both of his hands and sweep with his right thigh, throwing Derrick as shown. This is a high amplitude throw and is effective.

Hand Prop Throw

This is a great way to throw your opponent suddenly and pick up some points along the way. It's also ideal as a takedown to get him to the mat and finish him. Kolden is using his right hand and arm to hook under Kevin's left shoulder.

Kolden lowers his body level by bending his knees and starts to drive toward Kevin as shown. Kolden starts to grab for Kevin's right leg with his left hand.

Kolden runs past Kevin and places his left hand on Kevin's right knee at the side of the knee as shown. As he does this, Kolden uses his right shoulder to wedge tightly into Kevin's left upper chest as shown. This combination of a low grip (at the knee) and a high grip (at the shoulder and chest) is a classic example of the "high and low" control you need for leg grabs or ankle picks.

Pick Ups and Leg Grabs

Kolden really drives hard as he uses his left hand to prop or block on the outside of Kevin's right knee.

By running across the front of his body and propping Kevin's right knee with his left hand, Kolden throws Kevin.

Throws and Takedowns

Ankle Scoop Pick Up Throw

Bryan is on both knees and Drew is dominating him from a standing position. Bryan uses his right hand to grab high on Drew' left shoulder.

Bryan uses his right leg to drive between Drew's legs as he continues to pull on Drew's left shoulder with his right hand as shown. As he does this, Bryan uses his right hand to grab the front of Drew's right foot and ankle.

Bryan uses his right hand to pull Drew to his left front and as he does, Bryan uses his left hand to lift Drew's right foot and leg as shown. Bryan starts to stand as he does this.

Bryan uses his head on the back of Drew's shoulder to steer Drew over as Bryan continues to pull wit his right hand on Drew's shoulder.

Bryan keeps pulling with his right hand and lifting with his left hand and throws Drew.

Bryan lifts and throws Drew to the mat and finishes the throw.

Ankle Pick to Toehold

Jarrod, on the right, is tied up with Chris in a low, defensive posture.

Jarrod shoots in with his left foot and leg as shown and uses his left hand to grab Chris's right ankle. Notice that Jarrod has good control with his right hand on the Chris's head.

Throws and Takedowns

Jarrod pulls hard with his right hand on Chris's right ankle and pulls the ankle to his right hip as shown. This takes Chris to the mat quickly.

Jarrod plants Chris to the mat firmly and keeps control of Chris's right ankle wit his left hand.

Jarrod starts his toehold from this position.

Jarrod uses his right foot to step over Chris and secure the toehold tighter.

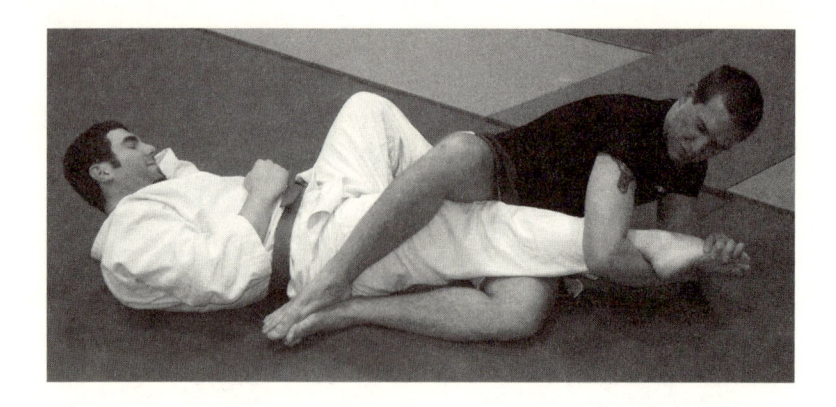

Jarrod may have to roll to his left side to get extra control and effect of the toehold to finish the move.

Pick Ups and Leg Grabs

Tight Waist and Crotch Lift

This throw is a powerful move that can certainly end a fight in a hurry. This is also an unexpected, and often successful, counter to an opponent who has dominated the grip and has you in a low, defensive posture. Chris, on the right, is crouched over and being dominated by Derrick's right hand on his back.

Chris uses his right foot to step in, and as he does, uses his right hand and arm to grab around Derrick's left hip and waist. Chris ducks his head under Derrick's right arm and jams his head up and into the back of Derrick's right shoulder as shown.

Throws and Takedowns

Chris uses his left arm to scoop up and through Derrick's crotch as shown. As he does this, Chris uses his right arm to tight waist Derrick.

This view shows how Chris has used his left hand to scoop up through Derrick's crotch and used his right arm to grab tightly around Derrick's left hip and waist. Notice how Chris has lowered the level of his body by bending his knees and keeping his back straight. Chris wants to keep his upper body in line with his hips and not bend over at the waist for maximum stability and power.

Chris plants the right side of his head firmly on Derrick's right ribcage area and as he does, lifts Derrick up with his hands and arms. Chris starts to step in toward Derrick as he does this.

Here's another view of how Chris scoops Derrick and picks him up. Notice that Chris has a strong base with his legs and is using them to help him lift Derrick.

Chris scoops Derrick up with both hands as he uses his head to drive into Derrick's right side, throwing Derrick up and over his right shoulder.

Here is the throw at the peak of its effect.

Chris wheels Derrick over his right shoulder as shown.

Pick Ups and Leg Grabs

This shows how Chris is using his hands and arms to scoop and lift Derrick. Chris is using his right arm to control Derrick at the waist and using his left arm to control Derrick between his legs. Chris wheels Derrick up and over his right shoulder.

Chris finishes the throw by slamming Derrick flat on his back.

Hand Wheel

Mike, on the right, has a looping grip with his right hand over Drew's right shoulder.

Drew moves his body to his left (to the right side of Mike) and as he does, uses his right hand to grab high on Mike's left shoulder as shown. You can see how Drew is using his left hand to scoop between Mike's legs from the back and is grabbing Mike's right upper thigh near the crotch.

Pick Ups and Leg Grabs

Here's another view of how Drew has moved to his left and to the right of Mike's body. You can see how Drew is grabbing Mike's left shoulder on the jacket with his left hand. Drew is using his head to drive into the back of Mike's right shoulder and using his left hand to scoop between Mike's legs.

Drew throws Mike by pulling up and to the right with his right hand as he uses his left hand to scoop through Mike's legs. This causes Mike to be lifted up and thrown forward over his left shoulder.

Throws and Takedowns

Here is the throw at the peak of its effect.

Here's another view of this throw. Drew has picked Mike up and is wheeling him over. To get more force in the throw, Drew can walk forward or even use either of his feet or legs to prop Mike more or use a thigh lift. There are a lot of variations of this throw, so don't hesitate to experiment with them.

SECTION FOUR
Knee Drop Throws

"Skill is the practical application of technique."
Steve Scott

Throws and Takedowns

IMPORTANT POINTS ABOUT KNEE DROP THROWS

I like knee drop throws because they have a high ratio of success and are hard to counter. Knee drop throws have an important place in the arsenal of many grapplers, including those who have trained with me and are common in sambo, judo and sport jujitsu. This section of the book presents a good many knee drop applications and it's hoped that you can use what's presented here as a good source of technical information on this phase of throwing for a long time to come.

An effective knee drop, especially one that is done with the attacker turning his back to his opponent operates on several key principles. They are:

1. Stability. The attacker is on a stable base (both knees).

2. Center of Gravity. The attacker drops below his opponent's center of gravity. Much like someone who is running would trip over a low fence below his line of sight at the waist or lower, you drop below your opponent's center of gravity, upsetting his balance forward.

3. Rotation. The attacker quickly rotates as he drops below his opponent's center of gravity and pulls him forward into the direction of the throw and over his own body. This action of rotation, along with dropping below your opponent's center of gravity causes a great amount of momentum and force into the action of the throw.

While knee drops are excellent throws, I've always believed that you should use them judiciously. It's like a "change up" pitch in baseball. An effective knee drop attack is unexpected. If you keep hitting one knee drop attack after another, they lose their sting and surprise value. Also, knee drop throws bridge the gap between a throw and a takedown. Sure, you're trying to slam your opponent for maximum points with a knee drop throw, but if the referee gives you a lesser score or if you don't throw him cleanly, you still pretty much have him down on the mat and you can follow up with a pin or submission hold. One of the knee drops shown later in this book is a move designed to slam your opponent flat on his face and front side and soften him up so you can immediately follow up with a pin. My wife Becky (the first American woman to win a World Sambo Championship) used this move with effective results, as did her friend AnnMaria (Burns) DeMars, the first American to win a World Judo Championship. Becky would often knock her opponent to her front side, then quickly get her hooks in and score with a choke (if she was doing judo) or follow up after the throw for a hold-down (if she was doing sambo). AnnMaria would often say that her ultimate goal was to get her opponent to the mat and either pin or armlock her. Her most-often used way to do it was her version of her knee drop shoulder throw. Critics would often comment on the lack of aesthetics in doing these moves, but the critics weren't the ones winning world titles.

Knee drops are useful for any type or size of athlete, male or female. I'm 6'4" and used knee drop throws effectively as an athlete, and my wife Becky, who is 5"3", used them as well. Opponents are often caught unaware by the suddenness of you dropping under them and throwing them over your body, especially if you're taller than they are.

To an untrained eye, many of the knee drop throws look alike, but each is different in the set up, as well as application of the throw. Like any other type of throwing technique, the attacker's grip, along with his control of the distance between his body and his opponent's, as well as body movement offers different opportunities for different knee drops. Basically, a knee drop throw is when you drop under your opponent's center of gravity and roll him over your body with control and force, but the different grips make each knee drop throw a bit different. You may roll him over your back, hip or shoulders, but you still are rotating him over your body with control and force. Basically, I'm showing the same attack pattern from a variety of different situations, grips and set ups. As I said before, it may all look like the same throw to an untrained eye, but when you seriously study knee drops, you will see the many obvious, and subtle, differences between each knee drop throw shown here. By the way, the knee drops shown on these pages are not the final word on the subject. Use your imagination and experiment with the many different grips, postures and set ups that you can use to make a knee drop work for you.

Before going into the specifics of the various knee drops, some core, fundamental points are presented.

Screw Yourself Into the Mat

The best way to get under your opponent's center of gravity, turn your body and get into a stable position on both knees is to "screw yourself into the mat." While this is a weird description of how to get into proper position to throw your opponent, it really does describe exactly what you do if you perform this move right. This photo shows Steve starting his knee drop attack and how he will screw himself into the mat.

Steve is making 180 degrees rotation with his body and lowering it under Mike's center of gravity, all in one split second. This is the actual "screwing into the mat" that you have to do to make this move work.

Throws and Takedowns

Steve's knees are pointed to his left and his butt is pointed to the right. By screwing himself into the mat, Steve has successfully dropped under Mike's center of gravity and pulled Mike forward and into the direction of the throw with the rotation of Steve's body. Also notice that Steve is "round" and rolling Mike over his body. This explosive rolling, round movement under your opponent's center of gravity is the most efficient way of throwing your opponent in a knee drop throw.

Split His Legs

When you hit in for your knee drop, roll in a really compact ball (be round) and shoot in as far as possible between his legs. This is what we call "splitting his legs" and the deeper you are between them, the more his legs will split and the better the throw! You can see how Mark's knees are pointing to his left and his hip and rear end is pointing to the right in this photo. The combination of Mark being under his opponent's center of gravity, along with his body rotating in the direction of the throw (screwing himself into the mat) and having his body so deep under Kirk's base (his legs) is the action that will throw Kirk over Mark's body.

Don't Flop and Drop

This is not the preferred position you should be in when doing a Knee Drop throw. This is what is often called the "flop and drop" and the name describes what really happens. All too often, grapplers drop themselves to the mat and land on their knees in the position that Ken is showing in this photo. When you do this, about the only way you can throw your opponent is to jack him up into the air and try to throw him directly forward. What happens often is that the attacker who did the flop and drop is driven forward to the mat by the defender and if the defender is thrown, he usually only lands on his face or shoulder and the effect of the throw is minimal. When you are kneeling directly in front of your opponent in this way, you are too vulnerable to being taken backward by your opponent. While some athletes have made this style of Knee Drop work for them, and other people may find this position aesthetically pleasing, I don't recommend it as it has a low percentage of success and requires far too much strength to throw someone.

Lock Your Opponent's Shoulder to Your Shoulder

Control your opponent's upper body to stabilize it so you can pull him over your body as you drop under him. In this case, Kevin is locking Kirk's shoulder to his shoulder to control the upper body, but you can use any part of his body using any grip that works so that you can lock his upper body onto your body as you drop below his center of gravity, screw yourself into the mat and drive him over your body with the Knee Drop throw.

Correct Finish for Knee Drop Throws

Finish your throw by driving hard into your opponent and put him on the mat flat on his back. You can see how Mark is driving hard with his left foot into the direction driving his upper body into his opponent. You can really splatter a guy with a knee drop and this photo shows it!

Incorrect Finish for All Knee Drops

Do not finish the knee drop this way. Mark is balled up and sitting on his knees with no follow-through at all. This is a weak finish and allows your opponent a chance to turn out or fall with less impact and this will lessen the effect of your throw and result in a smaller score. Finishing a knee drop in this way also gives your opponent a chance to stay on your back and hook his legs in to control you.

1-Arm Knee Drop (Pulling with Sleeve)

This version of the knee drop is out of a neutral grip where the attacker has his right hand on his opponent's left lapel and his left hand on his opponent's right sleeve. This is the first version of the Knee Drop that I teach.

Mark, on the right, and Roy both have a neutral grip in this photo. Each has his right hand holding the opponent's left lapel and his left hand holding his opponent's right sleeve immediately above the elbow at about the triceps.

Mark fits in for the throw as he uses his left hand to pull on Roy's right sleeve. Mark uses his right arm to hook under Roy's right shoulder. An important point in this throw is how Mark uses his right arm to cinch or squeeze Roy's right upper arm. Mark's right fist is pointing straight up and his right elbow is pointing to the mat. Mark uses his right hand to lock and squeeze Roy's right upper arm near the shoulder. Mark doesn't want to jam his right shoulder up and under Roy's right shoulder.

Knee Drop Throws

Mark "screws himself into the mat" as he locks his right shoulder to Roy's shoulder by cinching his right arm tightly onto Roy's right upper arm as shown. Mark spins on his right (lead) foot quickly as he turns his body into the throw. I call this movement the "roll" into the attack. As he does this, Mark quickly drops on both knees, making sure to have both of his knees pointing to his left and his buttocks sticking out to his right. By doing this, he has turned explosively around and "screwed himself into the mat."

Here is a side view of how Mark fits tightly in and under Roy and is under Roy's center of gravity.

Throws and Takedowns

Here is a side view of the peak of the throw's effect.

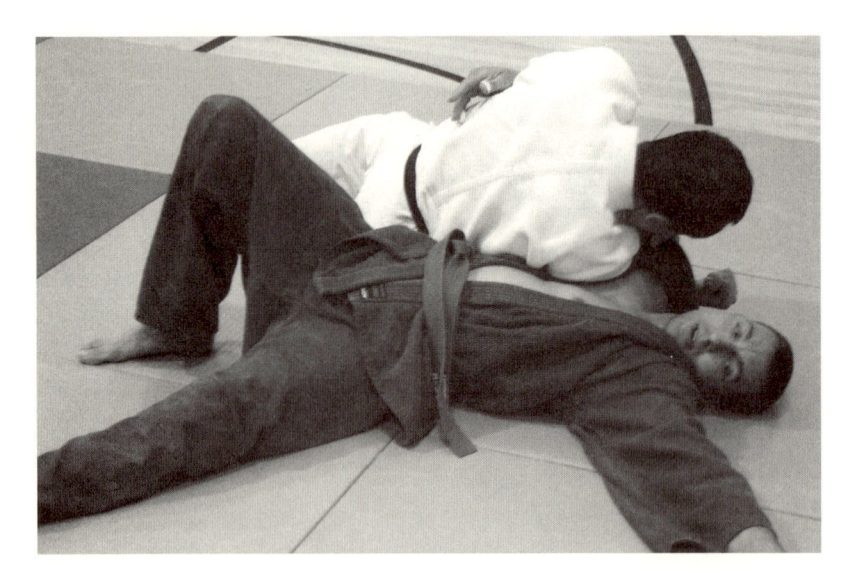

Here's the finish to this knee drop shoulder throw. Mark drives hard by extending his legs and driving his upper body into Roy to make sure Roy rolls over largely onto his back for a maximum score.

1-Arm Knee Drop (Pulling with Lapel)

In this version of the Knee Drop throw, Mark holds both of Roy's lapels as shown. Instead of using his left hand to pull on Roy's right sleeve, Mark will use his left hand to pull on Roy's right lapel. Doing this, gives Mark more control of Roy's entire right shoulder and upper body.

Here's a closer look at how the thrower uses his right arm to cinch his opponent's right shoulder tight to his own right shoulder. In this photo, Kevin has locked his right arm and shoulder firmly in place, squeezing Kirk's right upper arm between Kevin's right forearm and right biceps, ready to start his attack. There must not be any distance between your shoulders. Do not try to "jack up" your opponent with your shoulder either. You're not trying to throw him over your shoulder, but rather using your right shoulder to lock him into place so you can "roll" your body in for the throw. Kevin, as the attacker, wants his right shoulder locked tightly onto Kirk's for maximum control.

Mark fits in and cinches his right arm tightly to Roy's arm. Mark pulls hard with his left hand on Roy's right lapel. Doing this closes the distance between the upper bodies and locks Mark to Roy for better control.

As soon as Mark cinches Roy's right upper arm and shoulder, he screws himself into the mat and fits under Roy. Mark's knees are together and pointed to Mark's left with his buttocks pointed to his right.

Knee Drop Throws

Here's another view of how deep, compact and low you need to be when doing a good knee drop. Mark's body is under Roy's hips and center of gravity and deep under and between Roy's legs. Mark has Roy ready to throw.

Mark uses his left hand to pull on Roy's right lapel and as he does, curls forward and uses his right hand to steer Roy over his body. Mark wants to move his right hand over and across his body in the same way he would if he were swinging an ax chopping wood.

This photo shows Mark throwing Kirk and illustrates the "rolling action" of this throw. Remember, you don't want to lift or jack him up and over your body, but rather, scoop low and deep under your opponent and roll him over your body with speed, control and force. This photo shows how your opponent will roll over you and this is why it's vital to have a good finish to your knee drop throw.

As with all knee drops, the finish is crucial. Here's the finish to this knee drop shoulder throw with Mark driving hard into Roy to make sure Roy rolls over largely onto his back for maximum points.

Open Opponent's Base and Attack with Knee Drop

Ken's opponent, Scott, has his legs close together and Ken wants to widen Scott's stance so Ken can shoot under and throw. You don't always need to do this in Knee Drop throws, as the force and momentum of your low attack often forces your opponent's legs wide anyway. But, in some cases, you may need to open him up. To do this, Ken is using his right foot to slap, sweep or kick the inside of Scott's right foot and move it to Scott's right.

Ken uses his right foot to control Scott's right foot as shown and open his stance wide.

As soon as Scott places his right foot on the mat, Ken shoots in with his knee drop.

In this case, you can see that Ken is using his right hand to grab Scott's right upper sleeve. Ken has his left hand holding low on Scott's right sleeve.

Knee Drop Throws

Ken has screwed himself into the mat and is starting his throw.

Ken is throwing Scott and you can see how Ken is driving off his feet and knee into the direction of the throw.

Shoulder Grip Knee Drop Throw

Derrick is using his left hand to grab Sam's right shoulder at about the shoulder blade. Not many people expect a Knee Drop throw from this grip.

Here's another view of how Derrick is gripping Sam to start the throw.

Knee Drop Throws

Derrick uses his left hand to pull on Sam's right shoulder and as he does, Derrick starts his fit in for the throw.

Notice how close Derrick's right back shoulder is to Sam's right front shoulder as Derrick shoots in for the throw.

Throws and Takedowns

Derrick has screwed himself into the mat and loaded Sam on his back ready to throw him.

Derrick throws Sam and finishes the throw by driving into him to get maximum points.

Cross Arms Knee Drop

This is a great knee drop throw and was used by World Sambo Champion Becky Scott. Basically, you swing one of your opponent's arms under his other arm and he has no hands to stop the fall or even do a breakfall. This throw is a serious one and results in maximum points when you do it.

Mark is holding Kirk's sleeves with each of his hands as shown. An important point is that Mark's right hand is holding low (near the wrist) on Kirk's left sleeve and using his left hand to hold at about the elbow on Kirk's right sleeve.

Here's another view of how Mark controls Kirks using his sleeves.

As Mark fits in for the throw, he uses his right hand to swing Kirk's left arm under his right arm as shown. Mark is using his left hand to pull on Kirk's right sleeve at the elbow as shown.

Mark swings Kirk's left arm under his right arm as shown and screws himself into the mat for the knee drop. You can see how Kirk is really loaded up on Mark's back and Kirk's hands and arms are completely controlled.

Knee Drop Throws

Mark continues to use his right hand to drive Kirk's left arm up and under his right armpit so that Kirk's left hand is pointed out to Kirk's right side. Doing this really traps Kirk's left arm up and across his own body making it totally useless.

Mark makes sure to really rotate his body to the right front as he uses both hands to pull Kirk over.

This is a hard fall for Kirk to take as both of his arms are tied up and he has nothing to use to break his fall with. Kirk will land hard flat on his back.

Mark throws Kirk very hard flat on his back.

The momentum of the throwing action causes Mark to land on Kirk and he's ready to follow through with a pin.

Lapel and Sleeve Swing Knee Drop

This series of photos shows how a taller athlete can successfully use knee drops on his opponent.

Steve, on the right, is grabbing Mike with his left hand on Mike's right lapel and is using his right hand to grab low on Mike's left sleeve.

Steve opens Mike up by using his left arm to pop Mike's right arm up. This creates an opening for Steve.

Steve uses his right hand to swing Mike's left arm under his right armpit as shown. As he does this, Steve uses his left hand to pull hard on Mike's right lapel.

As Steve swings Mike's left arm under his right arm, he screws himself into the mat explosively.

Steve is on both knees, making sure both of his knees are pointing to his left and his buttocks is pointing to his right as shown. Steve continues to pull with his left hand on Mike's lapel as he rotates under Mike.

Here's another view of how Steve is under Mike's center of gravity and at the peak of the throw.

Knee Drop Throws

Steve throws Mike flat on his back.

Both Sleeves (Arm In) Knee Drop

This is an effective knee drop throw and was used by World Sambo Silver Medal winner Warren Frank in both his sambo and judo career.

Mark, on the right, is grabbing each of Kirk's sleeves as shown.

Mark uses his right hand to cross Kirk's left arm over his right arm as shown.

Knee Drop Throws

Mark continues to swing Kirk's left arm out and forward as he uses his left hand to tuck and pull on Kirk's right sleeve. As he does this, Mark drops under Kirk as shown.

Here's another view of how Mark is using both sleeves and how he has dropped under Kirk.

Throws and Takedowns

Mark throws Kirk over his body.

Mark finishes the throw.

Both Sleeves (Arm Out) Knee Drop

This is a variation of the both sleeves throw where the attacker has his right arm outside of the defender's left arm.

Mark is grabbing both of Kirk's sleeves as shown.

Mark fits in for the throw and uses is right arm on the outside of Kirk's left upper arm as shown to swing Kirk's left arm up and forward.

Throws and Takedowns

You can see how Mark is using his right arm on the outside of Kirk's left arm controlling the sleeve. Mark is using his left hand to tuck and pull on Kirk's right arm as shown.

It's important in this knee drop variation for Mark to have a strong rotation of his body as he screws himself into the mat. Look at how Mark's knees are both pointed to his left and he is throwing Kirk over his back as much as over his right hip. Mark is using his right hand on Kirk's left sleeve to steer him over as he pulls him.

Knee Drop Throws

Here's the throw at the peak of its effect. Notice how Mark is using his right hand to drive Kirk over and using his left hand to wrap and pull.

Mark's strong momentum and rotation causes him to land on Kirk as he finishes the throw.

Both Arms Knee Drop

This is a standard and common version of the Knee Drop (Morote Seoi Nage in judo) and is a powerful one.

Kirk and Mark are in a neutral grip with the right hands on the lapels and the left hands on the sleeves.

Kirk uses his left hand to pull up and out on Mark's right sleeve at the elbow as shown, as he uses his right arm to jam under Mark's right armpit.

Knee Drop Throws

Kirk continues to pull and jam his right arm under Mark's right armpit as he screws himself into the mat. Kirk's right hand (holding Mark's left lapel) is straight at the wrist and curls Mark's lapel giving Kirk more stability and power with his right hand.

Kirk continues to pull hard with his left hand on Mark's right sleeve as he throws Mark.

Kirk finishes the throw.

2 on 1 Lapel Knee Drop

This is similar to the previous throw, except that Kirk is using his right hand to hold onto Mark's right lapel as shown.

Kirk fits into the throw and uses his left hand to pull hard on Mark's right sleeve. Kirk uses his right hand (holding Mark's right lapel) to pull and starts to bend it at the elbow.

Throws and Takedowns

Kirk is using his right arm and elbow to jam under Mark's right shoulder at the armpit as shown. Kirk continues to pull with his left hand as he fits into the throw.

Kirk quickly rotates and screws himself into the mat with both knees pointing to Kirk's left and his buttocks to his right.

Knee Drop Throws

Kirk continues to pull and throws Mark. Here is the throw at the peak of its effect. Notice that, like most every other knee drop, this is a powerful and hard throw.

Kirk finishes the throw. Kirk's momentum into the throw causes his body to drive into Mark as he follows through.

Tight Waist (Hip Throw) Knee Drop

This is a useful, but not very common, variation of the Knee Drop. I like it because it gives the thrower a lot of control of his opponent's hips.

Mark, on the right, and Roy are holding each other in a neutral grip.

Mark uses his right hand and arm to reach around Roy's waist.

Knee Drop Throws

Mark uses his right hand to reach around Roy's waist as far as possible as he screws himself under Roy's center of gravity. In this throw, it's important for Mark to really shoot his right hip in as far as possible.

Mark uses his left hand to pull hard on Roy's right sleeve as Mark rolls Roy over his body. This really is a sudden, hard throw and totally unexpected as it's not a common attack.

Back Grip Knee Drop

Chad is using his right hand to reach over Brian's left shoulder and grab Brian's belt. If Chad can't reach the belt, he can grab low on Brian's jacket.

Chad swings in and uses his left hand to pull on Brian's right sleeve as shown.

Knee Drop Throws

Chad screws himself into the mat and points both his knees to his left and his buttocks to his right as he pulls Brian over his hip.

Chad rolls Brian over his body and continues to roll on top of Brian to finish the throw.

Looping Grip Knee Drop

This is a good attack when your opponent is defensive and has his buttocks stuck out far away as Brian (on the left) is doing. Chad uses his right hand and arm to reach over Brian's right shoulder and grab Brian's belt (or low on his jacket) as shown.

Chad closes the space between his body and Brian's by pulling on Brian with both hands. Notice how Chad is tight contact with his right armpit and upper chest on Brian's right shoulder and back, making sure Brian's right shoulder is wedged under his right armpit. Now, Chad knows Brian is in close enough to attack him with the throw.

Knee Drop Throws

Chad fits in for the throw as shown here.

Chad screws himself into the mat and uses both hands to pull on Brian.

Throws and Takedowns

The explosive rotation and dropping below Brian's center of gravity throws him. Notice how Chad is using his right hand to pull on Brian's belt to help pull him over.

Chad finishes the throw by rolling over on top of Brian to get maximum points.

Head and Arm Knee Drop

Chad uses his right hand to reach around and grab Brian's collar as shown.

Chad fits in to the attack as he uses his right hand and arm to reach around Brian's head and grabs his right shoulder. Chad is using his left hand to pull hard on Brian's right sleeve.

Throws and Takedowns

Chad screws himself into the mat, using his left hand to pull hard on Brian's right sleeve and his right hand to control Brian's head as he throws him.

Chad finishes the throw by landing on top of Brain and immediately pinning him.

Arm Wrap Knee Drop

Brian (on the left) is very defensive and backing away from Steve.

Steve uses his left hand on Brian's sleeve to pull Brian's arm into Steve's chest as shown in this photo. Steve uses his right hand to reach over Brian's right shoulder. Steve leads with his right foot and places it close and on the inside of Brian's right foot.

Throws and Takedowns

Steve uses his right hand to grab and hook over Brian's right shoulder and grab in his armpit. Steve is using his left hand on Brian's sleeve to trap Brian's right arm to Steve's chest.

Steve uses his right hand and arm to control Brian's right shoulder and arm as he attacks with the Knee Drop throw.

Leg Hooks and Sweeps

Here is a photo of how Steve's body is fit in for the throw.

Steve pulls hard and rolls Brian over and lands on him to finish the throw.

Throws and Takedowns

Face First Knee Drop

This was a favorite of Becky Scott, who won a lot of matches with this throw. It's a rough throw and your intention is to throw your opponent face first onto the mat and soften him up for a follow up with a ground attack. If you get points for it, great, but the idea is to get him down and throw him on his front side and face.

Steve uses his left hand to grab Brian's left lapel about midway down his chest.

Leg Hooks and Sweeps

Steve uses his right hand to grab Brian's left lapel immediately above his right hand as shown.

Steve uses his left hand to pull on Brian's left lapel and uses his right hand to curl up under Brian's left lapel as he swings in for the knee drop.

Throws and Takedowns

Steve screws himself into the mat as he uses both hands to pull on Brian's left lapel. Notice that Steve's right hip isn't in as deep as usual for most knee drops.

Steve pulls Brian hard with both hands on his left lapel and throws Brian onto the mat face first and onto his front side.

Steve really drives Brian hard onto the mat.

Steve immediately follows through with a pin or other groundfighting move.

Fireman's Carry

The Fireman's Carry or Shoulder Wheel throw is another way of doing a knee drop. The only differences are that you don't screw yourself into the mat and turn in a 180 degree rotation and that you are carrying your opponent over your shoulders rather than your upper back and hip as done in the other knee drop applications.

Drew (right) is on both of his knees and being dominated by Chas.

Drew quickly pops up to both of his feet (to get points for throws in judo and often in sambo, you have to start the attack on your feet).

Drew uses his left hand to pull on Chas's right sleeve as he swings his body in and drives his right knee between Chas's legs. Drew uses his right hand to scoop up and through Chas's legs and grabs Chas's right leg.

Throws and Takedowns

Drew uses his left hand to pull down and to his left on Chas's right sleeve and drives his right shoulder hard into Chas's stomach.

Drew wheels Chas over his shoulders as shown.

Leg Hooks and Sweeps

You can see how Chas is falling over his right shoulder and toward Drew's front left corner.

Drew finishes the throw with Chas flat on his back.

Fireman's Carry Front Drop

Drew shoots in for the Fireman's Carry, but in this variation, he will throw Chas directly to Drew's front side.

Knee Drop Throws

Drew uses both hands to lift Chas up and onto Drew's shoulders and upper back as he dips his head forward and throws Chas to his right side.

Drew throws Chas onto his back for maximum points and follows through with a pin or other ground move.

Fireman's Carry from a Cross Grip

Nikolay (on the left) has used his left hand to grab above Josh's left elbow on the sleeve as shown. Nikolay adds some control by using his head to push down on Josh's left shoulder and sucks Josh's shoulder in tight to him. This creates a "hole" under Josh's left armpit for Nikolay to swing under.

Nikolay drops on both knees as he shoots his head and body into the "hole" he created under Josh's left armpit. Notice how tight with his left hand and arm Nikolay has scooped Josh's left arm for control. Nikolay has used his right hand and arm to scoop up under and between Josh's legs.

Here's another view of how Nikolay has shot under Josh's body and is about to throw him.

Nikolay drives to his left rear corner as he uses his left hand to pull and scoop Josh's left arm and shoulder. Nikolay drives with the back of his head into Josh's body.

Throws and Takedowns

Nikolay drives hard to his left rear corner and throws Josh.

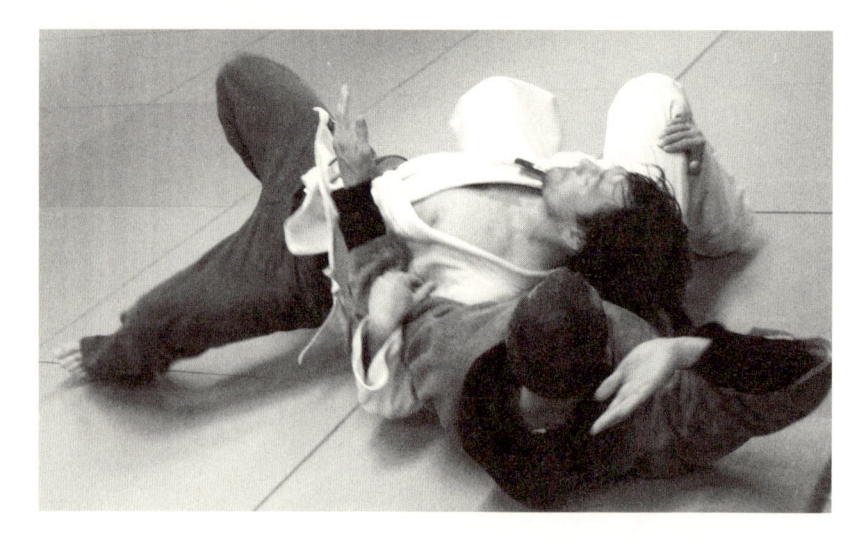

The explosive force and drive of Nikolay's attack throws Josh onto his back. Notice how Nikolay continues to drive with his upper body into the throw to finish the throw with maximum force and control.

Fireman's Carry Shoulder Shoot

Nikolay (left) is using his left hand to hold onto Josh's right sleeve at the elbow. Nikolay leads with his left foot.

Nikolay uses his left foot to step to the outside of Josh's right foot and leg as shown as he lowers his level and starts to scoop with his right hand.

Throws and Takedowns

Nikolay drives under Josh and wedges his right shoulder into Josh's midsection as he uses his right hand to grab around Josh's right upper leg. Nikolay's left leg is extended and fairly straight and his right knee is bent and Nikolay is sitting on his right side.

Nikolay uses his left hand on Josh's right sleeve to wheel him over and uses his right hand to hold and control Josh's right upper leg. Josh is being thrown over his right shoulder, but mostly over his head.

Knee Drop Throws

Nikolay keeps driving Josh over forward and onto his back.

Here's the finish of the throw.

Grabbing Your Opponent's Leg

Every grappler has his own preference for how he grabs his opponent's leg or scoops under his opponent's leg in a Fireman's Carry throw or takedown. This version shows Drew using his right hand to grab immediately above Chas's right knee. Use your imagination and experiment with how you may want to better control your opponent's lower body and legs when using the Fireman's Carry.

Look at how Chris has used his left hand and arm to grab under Bill's right knee. Chris has "snaked" or laced his right arm on his opponent's right (near) leg rather than hook under Bill's far leg. This is another way of controlling your opponent's lower body in the Fireman's Carry.

Drew is using his right arm to scoop up and between Chas's legs at the crotch. Hooking your arm through your opponent's crotch like this will soften him up and assist in throwing him.

Fireman's Carry Knee Drop

Here is a throw that's part knee drop and part fireman's carry, so I'm including it as the last throw in this section. Jarrod (left) has a 2 on 1 sleeve grip on Brian.

Jarrod keeps a good hold with his left hand low on Brian's right sleeve and uses his right hand to grab Brian's right lapel as shown.

Knee Drop Throws

As Jarrod fits in for the throw, he uses his right hand to pull Brian's right lapel and uses his left hand to pull on Brian's right sleeve.

Jarrod drops under Brian as shown as he ducks his head under Brian's extended right arm, all the while continuing to pull with both hands. Notice that Jarrod's left hip is closer to Brian and placed in front of Brian's right leg.

Jarrod pulls with both hands and pulls Brian over his shoulder as shown.

Here's the throw at the peak of its effect. Notice how Jarrod is driving almost directly to his right side as he pulls on Brian with both hands.

Knee Drop Throws

Jarrod drives hard and throws Brian flat on his back.

Throws and Takedowns

SECTION FIVE
Leg Hooks and Sweeps

"Function dictates form."
Louis Sullivan

Throws and Takedowns

Using your hips, leg, thigh, knee or foot to throw your opponent is a natural and effective way of throwing him. Whether you hook him with your leg, or use your leg or foot to sweep his feet out from under him, the same mechanical and technical principles of throwing him come into play. Your opponent's lower body is being thrown at a different speed than his upper body. This upending action is the basis of why these throws work.

Leg Hooks come in four basic varieties:

1. You use your leg to hook or reap your opponent across or to the outside of his body. In other words, you use your right leg to hook his right leg and throw him.

2. You use your right leg to hook or reap, to the inside of your opponent's stance, his left leg.

3. You use your right leg or foot to hook, reap or sweep your opponent's left leg across or outside of your opponent's stance.

4. You use your right leg or foot hook, reap or sweep your opponent's right foot or leg inside of your opponent's stance.

Leg, Foot or Thigh Sweeps are very much timing movements. Learning how to do a foot sweep on an opponent takes a lot of time, patience and practice. It's best to remember that foot, leg or thigh sweeps are "timing" throws where your control of your opponent's movement is vital to success. Good, effective foot sweeps are often hard to learn for some people simply because you are required to use precise timing when attacking your opponent. Your movement, and how you control the movement of your opponent is essential in these throws. However, they are worth the time and effort to master. If you have good timing and "good feet" you will throw a lot of opponents.

Cross Body Outer Hook Throw (No Jacket)

Alan (right) is using his right hand and arm to hook under Chuck's left shoulder. Note the position Alan's body is in and his stance in relation to Chuck.

Alan steps across Chuck with his left foot and leg as shown as he uses his left hand to scoop Chuck's right elbow in tightly to Alan's chest. Alan keeps good control with his right hand under Chuck's left shoulder. Notice that Alan's head is driving in the direction of the throw.

Leg Hooks and Sweeps

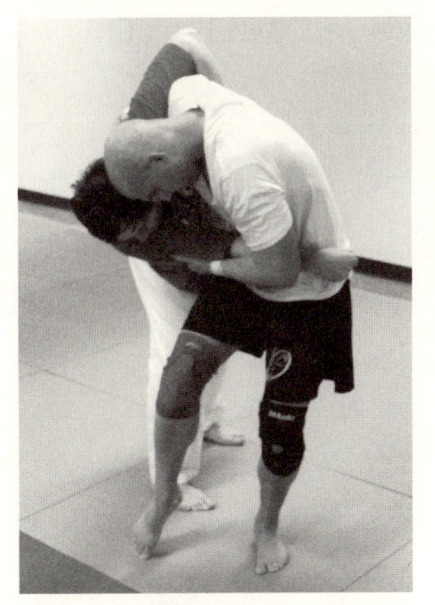

Alan's left foot (planted on the mat) is pointing in the direction he will throw Chuck. As Alan continues to scoop in with his left hand on Chuck's right elbow, Alan starts to hook with his right leg. Alan is pointing the toes on his right foot to that his right leg is cocked and ready to hook Chuck's right leg tightly and with control.

Alan uses his right leg to hook Chuck's right leg and throws Chuck to Chuck's right side as shown. Notice how Alan is driving forward with his head and his whole body is committed to the throw.

Alan throws Chuck hard on the mat.

Cross Body Outer Leg Hook (Lapel and Back Grip)

Steve (right) is gripping Roy with his left hand on Roy's right lapel and his right hand is gripping behind Roy's left shoulder on the jacket.

Steve steps sideways across the front of Roy's body as he uses his left hand to pull hard on Roy's right lapel. Steve uses his right hand, which is gripping Roy's left back and shoulder, to steer Roy into the direction of the throw. Here's a good illustration of how Steve pretends he has looped his belt around Roy's back and he is holding each end of the belt. Steve also makes sure to turn his right hip so that his right hipbone is aimed at Roy's front side.

Leg Hooks and Sweeps

Here's another view of how Steve's hands are working together to steer Roy to Roy's right and Steve's left and into the direction of the throw.

When Steve has stepped in front of Roy so that his left foot (on the mat) is directly in front of Roy's right foot, Steve uses his right leg to hook across Roy's right leg as shown. Notice that Steve's right foot is pointed down and the toes are leading the attack (Steve doesn't want to simply flop his right foot out or aim with his heel; he wants to aim with his toes for better control and power).

Steve uses his right leg to hook Roy hard and throw him flat on his back.

Cross Body Outer Leg Hook (Double Lapel Grip)

This is the same throw as the previous one only this time Steve is using a double lapel grip.

This shows how Steve has turned his hips so that he is turned and ready to attack as he steps with his left foot, moving across the front of Roy's body

Throws and Takedowns

Here's a view of how Steve uses both of his hands to control the grip on Roy's lapels. Look at how Steve is using his right hand and forearm on the front of Roy's left chest and pectoral area as he uses his left hand to move to the left.

This shows how Steve crosses in front of Roy and uses his right leg to hook sideways across Roy's right leg. You can see why it's important for Steve to have already turned his hips to his left so that he opens up his body and can hook Roy more easily and with better control

Here's the throw at the peak of its effect.

Leg Hooks and Sweeps

Sweeping Hip Throw

This is a classic throw used in judo, sambo and many styles of jujitsu and grappling.

Roman is breaking Drew's balance by "opening up" Drew's chest using his left hand to pull and using his right hand to pull forward also.

As Roman turns his hips to fit in for the throw, he continues to pull hard on Drew's right sleeve with his left hand. Roman has now used his right hand to grab behind Drew's upper back.

Throws and Takedowns

Roman has rotated in front of Drew as he pulled with his left hand on Drew's sleeve and is sweeping with his right leg across Drew's leg immediately above the knee. Look at how Roman is using his right hand to help pull Drew in and steer him.

Here is the throw at the peak of its effect.

Leg Hooks and Sweeps

Roman has thrown Drew to the mat and can go for a ground technique or remain upright. In the rules of sambo, if you throw your opponent to the mat with control and force and remain upright, you score a "Total Victory." This ends the match immediately and demonstrates that you have complete control over your opponent by throwing him and remaining balanced after the throw as well. This is the similar to an "Ippon" in sport judo.

Side Sweeping Hip Throw

This throw is pretty much a combination of the Cross Body Outer Leg Hook and the Sweeping Hip throw. Josh is using his left hand to pull on Nikolay's right lapel and is using his right hand to hold Nikolay's left back shoulder.

Josh steps to his left across Nikolay's body and pulls with both hands in the direction he is stepping.

Josh continues to step and starts to use his right leg to sweep across Nikolay's right front hip and leg.

Leg Hooks and Sweeps

Here's the leg placement of Josh's right leg across and slightly to the side of Nikolay. Josh continues to use both hands to pull.

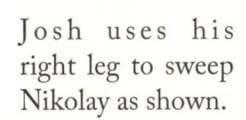

Josh uses his right leg to sweep Nikolay as shown.

Here's the throw at its peak. Nikolay will land hard on his back.

Outer Hook from the 2 on 1 Tie Up

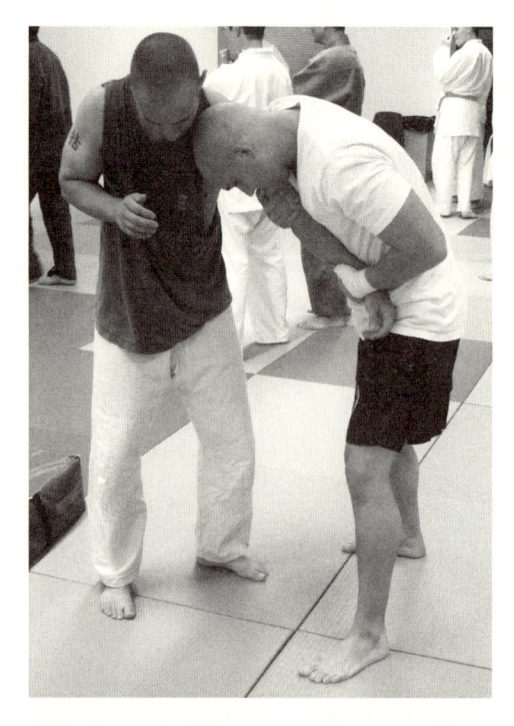

Alan has a 2 on 1 tie up on Kyle's left arm as shown. Look at how Alan is using his head to drive down on Kyle's left shoulder for more control.

Alan steps across Kyle's body with his left foot as shown and drives forward with his head for more control.

Leg Hooks and Sweeps

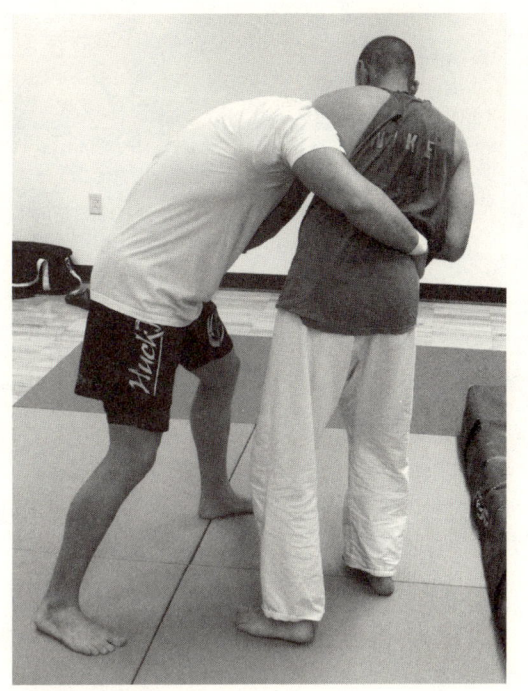

This view shows how Alan is using his right hand to reach around and tightwaist Kyle for more control.

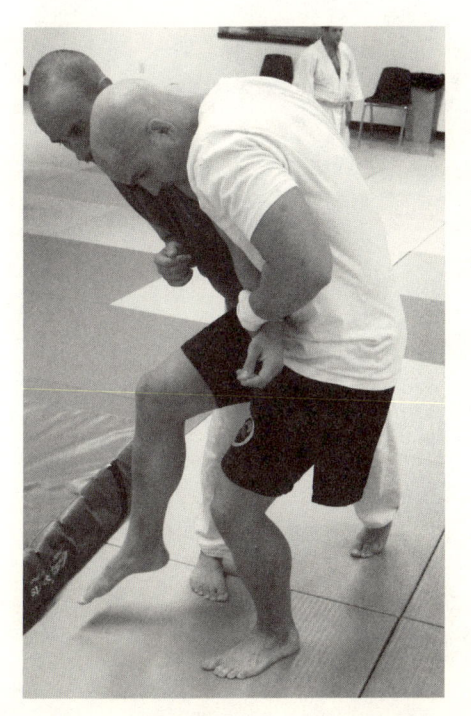

Alan uses his right leg to hook Kyle's right leg. Notice the pointed toes on Alan's right foot.

Throws and Takedowns

Alan uses his right leg to hook across Kyle's right upper leg immediately above Kyle's right knee as shown. Look at the control Alan has in this throw where Alan has locked his body onto Kyle's and has complete control of it.

Here's the throw at the peak of its effect.

Alan throws Kyle flat on his back to finish the throw.

Outer Hook from an Overhook

Kyle has Alan tied up with a double overhook grip and has his head placed on Alan's right shoulder as shown. Kyle is leaning forward and looking down at his left foot to break Alan's balance.

Kyle leans forward forcing Alan to place most of his weight on his right foot. Alan's balance is broken to his right rear corner.

Leg Hooks and Sweeps

Kyle uses his right leg to hook Alan's right leg as shown.

Kyle throws Alan hard onto his back.

Throws and Takedowns

Inner Thigh Throw (High Collar Grip)

This is a classic throw used in judo and sambo, as well as many styles of jujitsu. This version is the basic approach to the technique. Don't let that fool you; this is a great throw, but it takes a good amount of time to get confident in it.

Ken, on the right, is holding Scott in a high collar grip with his right hand. Ken is using his left hand to hold Scott's right sleeve immediately above his elbow.

Ken uses his left hand pull up and forward on Scott as he uses his right leg to lightly step across Scott's body.

Ken continues to pull with his left hand as shown as he rotates into the throw by stepping in with his left foot. It's important for Ken to pull Scott up and onto his chest so that Scott's chest (and entire upper body) is locked onto Ken's upper right side as shown.

Ken continues to rotate and pull Scott up and onto his body.

Throws and Takedowns

Ken uses his right leg to sweep and catches Scott on one of his inner thighs. Ken's pull and rotation throw Scott up and over Ken's body.

The Inner Thigh Throw (Uchi Mata in Japanese) is a spectacular, and effective throw used in all weight classes by both men and women.

Ken finishes the throw.

Inner Thigh Throw (Attack Opponent's Leg)

This version of the Inner Thigh throw emphasizes two primary factors; your use of your right leg to attack your opponent's left leg and the hopping action that adds power and control to the throw.

Ken (right) is using his right hand to grab Scott's jacket at Scott's left shoulder on the back and is using his left hand to pull Scott's right sleeve into Ken's stomach.

Here's another view of how Ken grips Scott to set him up for this throw.

Notice that Ken's right foot is placed slightly inside and to the front of Scott's left foot and leg.

Ken pivots on his right foot and swings his left leg around behind him as he pulls Scott with both hands.

Ken plants his left foot on the mat as he continues to turn his body and pull Scott forward.

Ken uses his right leg to sweep Scott's left leg as Ken continues to turn and pull.

Ken uses his right leg to sweep Scott's left leg and as he does this, Ken starts to hop to his left rear on his right leg. Doing this forces Scott to be thrown forward and over Ken's right leg that is sweeping.

Here's the hopping action (what the Japanese call "ken ken.") Ken keeps hopping (it only takes a few hops to throw your opponent) and using his hands to pull.

Leg Hooks and Sweeps

Here's the throw at almost its peak. You can see how deep Ken is and how powerful his sweeping and lifting action of his right leg is.

Ken finishes the throw by flattening Scott.

Inner Thigh Throw (Lapel and Back Grip)

This version of the Inner Thigh throw emphasizes good control of your opponent's jacket. Josh (right) is using his left hand to grab Nikolay's right lapel and using his right hand to grab Nikolay's jacket at the back behind his left shoulder.

Josh fits in for the attack, and as he does, uses his left hand to pull Nikolay's lapel as shown. Josh uses his right hand to pull Nikolay into his chest so that Nikolay's body is solidly attached to Josh's.

Josh turns in for the throw and pulls with his left hand on Nikolay's lapel while using his right hand to pull Nikolay's body into the throw.

Leg Hooks and Sweeps

Josh starts to sweep with his right leg and catches Nikolay on the inner thigh (either thigh works). Josh will continue on and throw Nikolay. It's important to remember that when using the Inner Thigh throw, don't fret too much what your attacking leg does. Let it sweep naturally and be an extension of your hip and upper body.

Here's the throw at its peak. You can see how Josh's head and upper body are forward and his right leg is sweeping and controlling Nikolay's leg. For a good Inner Thigh throw, you have to finish by driving your head forward as your leg sweeps and lifts up.

Inner Thigh Throw from an Overhook

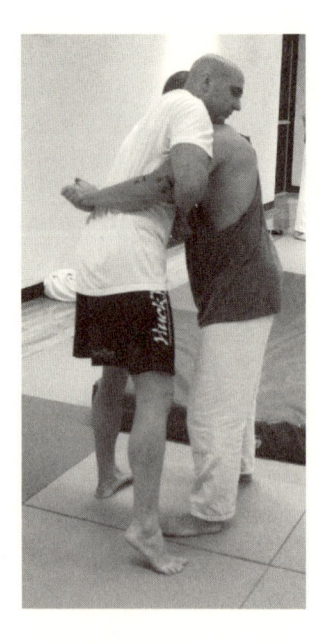

Alan is using both hands to hook over Kyle's arms immediately above Kyle's elbows. This version of the Inner Thigh throw is excellent for "no gi" situations and allows the attacker to have a lot of upper body control, which enables him to have a lot of lower body control as he fits in for the throw.

Here's another view of how Alan has tied up Kyle with his hooking arms. As Alan fits in for the throw, he starts to uses his right arm to hook a bit deeper under Kyle's left arm and shoulder.

Leg Hooks and Sweeps

Alan fits in for the throw and uses both arms to pull Kyle in hard to his body. You can see Alan starting to use his right leg to sweep inside Kyle's legs.

Alan pulls hard with both hands locking Kyle's upper body to Alan's. Alan drives forward into the movement of the throw and uses his right leg to sweep between Kyle's legs.

Here's the peak of the throwing action with Alan in full control.

Alan follows through and throws Kyle hard to the mat. Notice the use of crash pads in training. Crash pads reduce injuries and allow you to use full power when you practice your throws.

Inner Thigh Roll to Leglock

Josh (right) is using his right hand to grab over Ben's left shoulder and is using a back grip for maximum control. This pulls Ben in close to Josh's body tightly so Josh can quickly attack without having to close the space between his body and Ben's

Josh fits in for a forward throw as shown.

Here's a view of the powerful grip Josh has with his right hand over Ben's left shoulder and straight down Ben's back, grabbing his jacket.

Josh starts to roll forward over his left shoulder and as he does, he uses his right hand on Ben's jacket and back to pull hard. Josh also uses his left hand to grab the outside of Ben's left ankle as shown.

Josh rolls over his left shoulder as he uses his left hand to scoop Ben's left ankle. Josh uses his left hand to pull hard on Ben's jacket.

Leg Hooks and Sweeps

Josh rolls over his let shoulder bringing Ben with him.

Here's another view of this throw showing how Josh uses his right leg to sweep between Ben's legs and how Josh uses his left hand to control Ben's left ankle.

Throws and Takedowns

Josh rolls Ben over, keeping control of Ben's left ankle with his left hand.

Josh immediately applies a cross-body straight leglock.

Outer Leg Hook Against Opponent's Stiff Arms

When an opponent wants to avoid you and uses both of his arms to "stiff arm" you, it can be difficult to attack him.

Steve (right) is countering Drew's stiff arm defense by using his right hand to drive up on the inside of Drew's left arm as shown. Notice that Steve's right arm is bent at the elbow with his elbow pointed straight down and his hand pointed straight up to the ceiling.

Steve uses his right hand to drive over Drew's right shoulder as shown as he uses his left hand to pull on Drew's right sleeve and pull it to Steve's chest.

Steve uses his right hand to reach over Drew's right shoulder and grab either the belt of jacket near the belt. Notice that Steve's right foot is placed between Drew's feet.

Steve uses his left foot to step to his left as he uses his left hand to pull Drew's right sleeve to his body. Steve uses his right arm to cinch in tightly and control Drew's right shoulder.

Leg Hooks and Sweeps

Steve uses his right leg to hook Drew's right leg as shown, driving Drew to his left side.

Steve hooks hard with his right leg and throws Drew.

Steve finishes the throw as shown.

Throws and Takedowns

Hopping Outer Leg Hook Throw

This is a great attack when your opponent is bent over and has his hips far out and away from you.

Scott, on the left, is bent over in a defensive posture. Ken uses his right hand to get a back grip and uses his left hand to grab Scott's elbow and pull it in to his body.

As Ken continues to control Scott with his hands and grip, he pivots to his left on his base leg (his left leg and foot). As he does this, Ken uses his right leg to reach and hook Scott's right leg immediately above the knee. Look at how Ken is pointing his right foot with the toes down. Ken is using his right heel to hook to the outside and at the joint of Scott's right knee for maximum control.

Leg Hooks and Sweeps

Ken starts to hop around forward and in the direction of the throw with his left foot as shown. As he does this, Ken keeps his right foot locked onto the outside of Scott's knee to keep it from moving.

Here's another view of how Ken attacks Scott. You can see how Ken is using his right heel to hook to the outside and behind Scott's right knee. This keeps Scott from moving his right leg and locks Ken on tight to Scott.

Throws and Takedowns

As he continues to hop around and forward on his left foot, Ken sinks his right leg in deeper and continues to hook Scott's right leg as shown.

Ken continues to hop around forward, all the while, controlling Scott's leg (and entire body) more and more as he hops in.

Leg Hooks and Sweeps

Ken has hopped around to the side of Scott and has his left leg firmly planted on the mat as shown. Ken is using his right leg to hook hard on Scott's right leg and has his right foot pointed down to the mat for maximum power and control.

Ken hooks Scott with his right leg and throws him flat on his back.

Throws and Takedowns

Cross Grip Major Outer Hook

Not many opponents think you'll attack them with a cross body Major Outer Hook throw from this position and this element of surprise gives you an edge.

Steve (right) has a cross grip on Chad using his left hand to grab low on Chad's left sleeve immediately below Chad's left elbow.

Here's a view of how Steve uses his left hand to grip on Chad's left shoulder as he uses his left hand to grab Chad's left sleeve.

Leg Hooks and Sweeps

Steve steps forward and across Chad's body as shown. Steve uses his left hand to pull on Chad's left sleeve and as he steps in, Steve uses his right hand grip on Chad's back and shoulder to cinch his body in tight to the left side of Chad's body and left shoulder. Steve leans forward and into the direction of the throw with his body as he steps across the front of Chad's body.

As Steve drives across the front of Chad's body, he uses his right leg to hook Chad's right leg right above the knee. Steve's right foot is pointed down and he is using his foot to lock onto the outside leg at the knee joint.

Steve continues to drive forward hooking Chad's right leg with his right leg and throwing Chad.

Minor Inner Hook

This is a powerful throw and one that is hard to counter. My wife Becky (and many other athletes that I have coached) used this throw with great success in her career in both sambo and judo.

Derrick (right) has a neutral grip on Kyle. Derrick's right hand is holding Kyle's left lapel and Derrick's left hand in holding Kyle's right sleeve. I like to start this throw with this grip because is appears as if Derrick will use a right-handed attack on Kyle since he's using a conventional right grip. Usually, if you hold a right-sided grip such as this, you will use a right-sided throw. This variation of the Minor Inner Hook throw will be done from Derrick's left side, thus fooling Kyle. The throw will be done from a different angle in the following photos, but this angle shows you Derrick's lapel and sleeve grip more clearly than the other angle does.

Derrick steps back with his right foot and as he does, uses his right hand to pull on Kyle's left lapel. Derrick pivots on his left foot and swings his right foot and leg backward.

Derrick continues to use his right hand to pull on Kyle's left lapel while swinging his left hand down immediately above Kyle's left leg. It's important for Derrick to plant his right foot on the mat as shown (notice Derrick's right foot is sideways). Derrick's right foot almost square in front of and between Kyle's feet, so Derrick can drive hard directly into Kyle when he throws him. Derrick is also lowering his body by bending his knees. Derrick's stance is wide as shown.

Derrick drives into Kyle, using his left foot and leg to wrap on the inside of Kyle's left lower leg as shown. Notice how Derrick is driving off his right foot. Derrick makes it a point to use his head as a part of the throw and drives it into the left side of Kyle's chest. Derrick does not want to place his head under Kyle's left arm or armpit as it will lessen the power of the throw.

You can see the total commitment Derrick has in the throw. He is driving hard off his right foot, which is planted solidly on the mat, and has wrapped his left leg deeply around on the inside of Kyle's left leg. Notice that Derrick is pointing the toes on his left foot, giving him more power in the throw.

Derrick throws Kyle and lands on his left hip as shown. Don't try to land on your knee as it lessens the power and effectiveness of the throw.

It's important for Derrick to finish the throw by trapping Kyle's left leg and passing his guard so Derrick can immediately secure a hold-down. You don't want to get stuck between your opponent's legs in his guard, so make sure you finish the throw by trapping your opponent's leg and rolling over it to pass his guard.

Derrick finishes the move by getting past Kyle's left leg and securing a pin.

Minor Inner Hook from a Shoulder Throw

This is a good way to throw an opponent who has avoided your initial attack with a hop around defense.

Kirk is attacking Kevin with a right-sided Shoulder Throw.

Kevin avoids the attack by hopping to his right and Kirk's left. Notice that Kirk keeps control of Kevin's right upper arm by squeezing tight with his right arm and using his left hand to control Kevin's right elbow.

Leg Hooks and Sweeps

As Kevin completes his hop around movement, Kirk pivots on his right foot and swings his left leg backward.

Kirk plants his left foot on the mat as shown and lowers the level of his body by bending his knees. Kirk uses his right foot and leg to hook Kevin's right lower leg. Kirk is using his right arm to reach or scoop in for control.

Kirk continues to drive hard off his left foot as he uses his right leg to wrap around the inside of Kevin's right leg as shown. Notice that Kirk's right foot has its toes pointed, which gives more power in the throw. Kirk's head is turned and his right shoulder is driving against the right side of Kevin's chest. Kirk is using his right arm to grab Kevin's right leg.

Throws and Takedowns

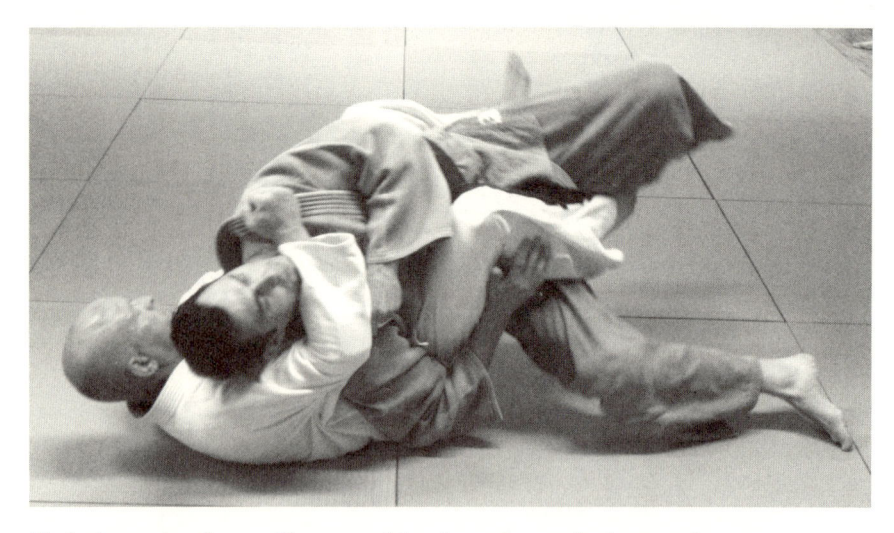

Kirk drives hard into Kevin and lands on his right hip as shown.

Kirk finishes the throw by driving really hard into the action of the throw so Kevin will land flat on his back. This variation of the Minor Inner Hook is popular in judo where you can get an Ippon (full point) and end the match by landing your opponent flat on his back.

Minor Outer Hook

Kevin, on the right, has Kirk in a cross grip.

Kevin closes the distance between his body and Kirk's by moving his right foot behind Kirk's body as shown. Kevin also makes sure to close the space between his upper body and Kirk's upper body. Kevin lowers the level of his body by bending his knees as shown. Make sure you do not bend over at the waist when you attack as this lessens your control and weakens the effect of your attack. An important point about doing an outer leg hook is don't be in a hurry to hook your opponent's leg. Lead the attack with your hip and commit your hip first before going for the outer leg hook. If you get in a hurry and stick your leg out to hook his leg before getting your hip in, your opponent can more easily counter you with an Inner Thigh throw.

Throws and Takedowns

Kevin uses his left hand on Kirk's left sleeve to drive forward into the direction of the attack. As he does this, Kevin places his head on Kirk's left shoulder as shown. Kevin's right hand continues to grab Kirk's left shoulder. Notice how Kevin has driven his body into the throw and is using his right foot to hook Kirk's right foot and leg.

Leg Hooks and Sweeps

Here's another view of the attack. Notice how Kevin is driving hard into the direction of the throw and is using his right leg to hook Kirk's far (right) leg. Kevin is using his right hand on Kirk's shoulder to drive harder and control the upper body.

Kevin fully commits his entire body into the throw and lands on his right hip throwing Kirk.

Minor Outer Hook with a Leg Grab

Kevin is using his left hand to grab immediately above Kirk's right (far) knee as he shoots in with his Minor Outer Hook. Doing this leg grab adds more control to the throw.

Major Inner Hook & 2-Arm Tackle from a Duck Under

John has Mike in a Russian 2 on 1 grip, but Mike is countering by using his left hand to push on John's head to create distance. John is leading with his right foot which is positioned between Mike's feet.

John uses his left hand to push or shuck Mike's right arm immediately above the elbow at the low triceps.

Throws and Takedowns

John ducks under Mike's left arm and uses his left foot to step into Mike, giving John a good stable leg. As John does this, he turns his body slightly so that his chest is flat against Mike's chest. John also starts to lower the level of his body by bending at the knees. Notice that John is starting to use his left hand to reach for Mike's left leg.

As John gets his head under Mike's left arm, he buries it hard against Mike's chest. As he does this, John uses his right leg to hook deeply between Mike's legs as shown. John drops low under Mike's center of gravity as he hooks with his right leg on Mike's left leg. Notice that John has used his left hand to grab immediately above Mike's left knee and John will use his left hand to scoop Mike's leg as he throws Mike backward. John also uses his right hand to grab around Mike's left hip and uses his left hand to scoop Mike at the buttock or upper thigh. This way, John is using his right leg to hook Mike's left leg and using both hands and arms to scoop and grab Mike's legs, throwing Mike with more control and force.

Leg Hooks and Sweeps

John has driven into Mike, landing on him chest to chest, and has thrown him flat on his back.

Hopping Major Inner Hook from a Cross Grip

This is an aggressive and unexpected attack from a cross grip. Steve is using his left hand to get the cross grip on Chad's left arm as shown. Steve is using his right hand to grab Chad's left shoulder at the jacket. Steve has controlled the cross grip and, after having done that, is leading with his right foot as shown.

Here's a back view of how Steve is using his right hand to grab Chad's left shoulder.

Leg Hooks and Sweeps

Steve explodes into the attack by using his right leg to hook Chad's left leg immediately above Chad's left knee. Steve can close the distance between his body and Chad's body by using his left foot to skip in toward Chad. Steve keeps his cross grip and makes sure that there is minimal (if any) space between his body and Chad's body.

Notice how Steve is using his right foot to hook Chad's left leg as he drives into Chad. It's important for Steve to get a good hook with his right foot and leg on the inside of Chad's left leg. This locks Steve's body onto Chad's body at the legs, while Steve locks his upper body onto Chad's upper body with his cross grip.

Throws and Takedowns

Steve aggressively drives into Chad with the attack and may have to hop in the direction of the throw with his left foot on the mat. Steve continues to use his right leg to hook Chad's left leg as he throws him. Steve drives Chad to the mat as shown.

Steve keeps using his right leg to hook as he drives into Chad with total commitment and throws Chad flat onto his back.

Change Direction Inner Leg Hook

This throw works because when you attack your opponent, you hook you leg to his leg and then change the direction of the throw.

Steve has Chad in a cross grip with his left hand low on the sleeve and his right hand grabbing Chad's left upper back and shoulder on the jacket. Steve's body is positioned to the outside of Chad's left foot and Steve is in a square stance.

Steve uses his right foot and leg to hook on the inside of Chad's left leg as shown. As he does this, Steve drives into Chad with his body.

Steve quickly changes the direction of his attack and uses his left foot to hop around to his left and in front of Chad. This hopping action gives Steve momentum into the throw. Look at how Steve uses his right foot to hook on the inside of Chad's left leg at about the knee and draw Chad's left leg into Steve. You can see how Steve's hooking action with his right leg on the inside of Chad's left leg widens Chad's stance and breaks his balance.

Steve immediately drives his body into Chad throwing Chad to his back.

Steve continues to drive into Chad, throwing him flat on his back.

Foot Kick Throw

This throw is also called the "Sticky Foot" because the attacker sticks his foot onto his opponent and controls him with it. Roman is using his left hand to draw Drew's left arm into a cross grip and is using his right hand to come over the top of Drew's left shoulder and get a back grip. Roman's right foot is immediately outside Drew's left foot as shown. Roman's body is firmly pressed close to Drew's for maximum control.

Roman pivots off his right foot and spins around so that his left foot is planted on the mat with his toes pointed in the same direction as Drew's toes. As he does this, Roman, uses his right foot to hook onto the back of Drew's left foot as shown. Notice how Roman is using the top of his right foot (at the shoe laces) to hook at the back of Drew's right heel. Roman's right knee is slightly bent as shown and Roman's right shin is firmly placed against the back of Drew's lower left leg. Roman continues to draw Drew in close to his body with his grip.

Leg Hooks and Sweeps

Roman continues to use his right foot and leg to hook at the back of Drew's left foot as Roman hops on his left foot around toward the front of Drew's body as shown. As he does this, Roman uses his left hand to pull on Drew's left arm and uses his right hand to pull Drew's body tight in as well. Roman is using his right foot to continue to hook and sweep with the top of his foot (at the shoelaces).

Roman continues to hop forward on his left foot around in front of Drew and starts the throw.

Roman continues to use his right foot to hook and sweep Drew's left foot as Roman uses his hips to turn into the direction of the throw. This control of Drew's left foot and ankle and the momentum created by Roman's hopping in a rotation around toward the front of Drew causes Drew to be thrown.

Roman finishes the throw by whipping his hips over and landing chest to chest on Drew.

SECTION SIX
Body Drop and Over Body Throws

"Throwing is the easy part. Getting into position the right way every time is the hard part."
Jerry Swett

Throws and Takedowns

Generally, these are the throws where the attacker keeps both of his feet on the mat as he attacks and throws his opponent. This gives the attacker real stability. Whether you throw him over your leg or hip isn't the defining feature of this type of throw. It's the fact that you are stable and usually on both legs as you throw him forward or to the side.

Body Drop throws are easily recognized. The attacker has his legs split apart and he throws his opponent over his body. A rule of thumb (and in important one) is for the attacker to make sure he has 50% of his weight on his right foot and 50% of his weight on his left foot. This can vary from person to person, but is generally true. Doing this gives you a stable base to attack and throw your opponent from. How far you split your legs apart is up to you. Some athletes use a wide split and get very low under their opponents, while others use a closer leg split. Experiment with what works best for you. The bulk of this section will be taken up with Body Drop throws.

Over Body throws are usually hip throws or any throw where the attacker throws his opponent up and over the attacker's body. Usually, the hip is the fulcrum for this to take place, but not always. It could be the upper or lower thigh or higher over the low back as well. Knowing how to engage with an opponent, turn your back to him and throw him up and over your body takes work. Often, these throws form the basis of how to throw with leg sweeps such as the Inner Thigh throw or Sweeping Hip throw. I'm presenting only a couple of Over Body throws in this section but that doesn't discount their effectiveness.

The Body Drop (Hook Opponent's Head)

Ken has a high collar grip with his right hand gripping the top of Scott's jacket. Ken's left hand holds Scott's right sleeve immediately above the elbow. Ken is leading with his right foot and has it placed on the inside and near Scott's left foot as shown.

Ken uses his left hand to pull up and forward on Scott's right sleeve and is using his right hand and arm to hook around Scott's head and neck. Ken pivots on his right foot and swings his left leg around behind this body.

Body Drop and Over Body Throws

Ken plants his left foot hard on the mat as he uses his left hand to pull up and forward on Scott's right sleeve. Ken uses his right arm to hook around Scott's head and neck as shown. Ken plants his right foot on the mat as shown. Ken's right foot is placed on the mat as shown with the heel up. Ken's right leg is mostly straight, but his right knee is flexed and slightly bent. The weight distribution is 50% on each foot.

Ken pulls hard in a snapping movement with his left hand as he flexes his right leg creating a springing action. All the weight in Ken's body is driving forward into the direction of the throw.

Ken slams Scott on the mat and finishes the throw.

Both Hands Body Drop

Roman (right) has a neutral grip on Nikolay and is in a square stance facing him. In this Body Drop, Roman will use a wide slip with his legs and shoot his right leg deep across the front and side of Nikolay's body.

Roman uses his left hand to pull hard on Nikolay's right sleeve as shown as he pivots on his right foot and swings his left leg around behind him.

Body Drop and Over Body Throws

Roman has swung around and places his left foot outside Nikolay's left foot as shown. As he does this, Roman uses his left hand to pull up and forward on Nikolay's right sleeve. Roman holds onto Nikolay's left lapel and swings his right arm and elbow up and under Nikolay's right armpit as shown. Roman's right leg is to the front and side of Nikolay's right leg and Roman is bending his right leg deeply. Notice Roman's right foot and how his foot is pushing off the mat at the toes.

This is a powerful throw and Roman pulls hard as he flexes up and forward with his lower body slamming Nikolay to the mat.

Open Chest Body Drop

Eric (right) is using his left hand to pull up and forward on Jarrod's right sleeve as shown. Eric uses his right hand to snap and pull up and forward on Jarrod's left lapel in much the same way you would flick your wrist when casting a fishing rod. As he does this, Eric uses his right foot to step between Jarrod's feet.

Eric uses his left hand to pull up and forward as he pivots on his right foot and swings his left foot and leg around behind him. Eric continues to "open" Jarrod's chest, using his hands. Remember, this throw works as well as it does because you are throwing your opponent up and over your body and not simply pulling him onto your body and locking him to it.

Body Drop and Over Body Throws

You can see how Eric's right hand is steering Jarrod's upper body by the use of his grip on Jarrod's left lapel. This shows how Eric is using his left hand to pull up and forward into the direction of the throw, breaking Jarrod's balance. Eric has planted his left foot on the mat and is about to place his right foot down in front of Jarrod.

Here's another view of how Eric fits into the throw.

Throws and Takedowns

Eric plants his right foot on the mat with the heel up and the knee pointed down toward the mat. This gives Eric a good spring or "flex" when he does the throw.

Eric throws Jarrod to the mat.

Back or Belt Grip Body Drop

This is a low, deep attack where you throw your opponent over your back and hip.

Chad (right) is using a back grip with his right hand reaching over Brian's left shoulder and gripping his jacket near the belt of actually grabbing Brian's belt. As Chad attacks, he places his right foot on the inside of Brian's right leg as shown.

Chad fits into the throw as he uses both hands to pull Brian to him and lock him onto his body. Look at the hip placement Chad has in this attack.

Chad continues to pull with both hands as he quickly rotates his body to his left. Chad shoots his right foot to his back and plants his right toes on the mat with his right heel pointed up. Chad's right knee is pointed down to the mat. Look at how Chad's hip is deeply fit in and Brian's body is being pulled over Chad's hip and lower back.

Chad is low, under Brian's center of gravity. He uses both hands to pull hard and roll Brian over his body, throwing him. Chad springs and flexes on his right bent knee giving this attack more forward momentum and power.

Chad throws Brian, landing on him.

2 on 1 Far Lapel Body Drop

Ken has Scott in a neutral right-handed grip as shown.

Ken quickly uses his right hand to let go of Scott's left lapel and grab Scott's right lapel as shown as he uses his left hand to pull on Scott's right sleeve. Ken swings into the throw as he does this.

Throws and Takedowns

Ken fits into the throw as he uses his right hand to grab Scott's right lapel as shown. Ken's right elbow is pointed down and his hand is pointed upward.

Ken fits in deeply and you can see how his right arm is jammed on the inside of Scott's right shoulder and under his right armpit. Ken has fit into the attack deeply and is using both of his hands and arms to pull on Scott's right side.

Body Drop and Over Body Throws

Here's the throw at the peak of its effect. This photo shows how Ken springs off his legs as he flexes his right leg.

Ken slams Scott to the mat and finishes the throw.

Throws and Takedowns

Side (Arm Trap) Body Drop

The direction of your attack can fool your opponent and this throw shows it. Jarrod (right) and Eric are in a neutral grip as shown.

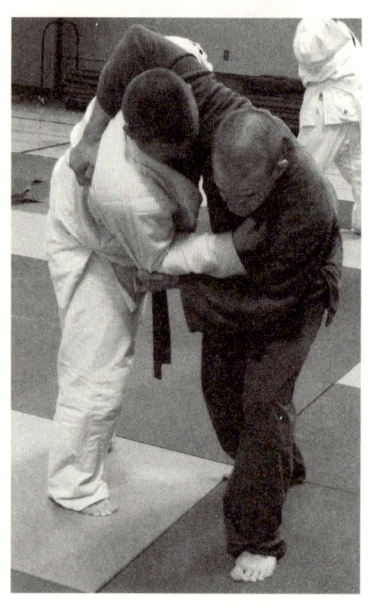

Jarrod turns his body quickly to his left and uses his left foot to step to his left as shown. Jarrod's placement of his left foot is important; it's placed out and in front of Eric's right foot as shown. Doing this gives Jarrod room to move. As he does this, Jarrod uses his left hand to pull in on Eric's elbow. Jarrod uses his right arm to reach over Eric's left shoulder and use a back grip. This movement breaks Eric's balance to his right side and Jarrod's left side.

Jarrod shoots his right leg across the side of Eric's right leg as shown. As he does this, Jarrod uses his right hand to pull down and in on Eric's right elbow. Jarrod uses his right hand to pull and lock Eric's body onto his.

Here's the throw at the peak of its effect.

Jarrod finishes the throw.

Back Grip Hip Throw

This is one of the primary throwing skills I teach and is often taught by many sambo coaches. It's a basic hip throw, but learning this is important to learning many fundamental skills in throwing someone forward over your body.

Steve (right) uses his right hand and arm to reach over Chad's left shoulder and grab either the belt or low on the jacket near Chad's belt. Steve uses his left hand to start to pull on Chad's right sleeve. Steve is stepping in with his right foot and will pivot on his right foot as he swings his left leg around and behind.

Steve has fit into the throw as he uses his left hand to pull up and forward on Chad's right sleeve at the elbow. You can see how Steve's right hand is grabbing deep down the middle of Chad's back. Steve has fit his right hip in front of Chad and will use it as a fulcrum to roll Chad over.

Body Drop and Over Body Throws

Here's another view of how Steve fits into the throw. Steve's hands and arms are working together and pulling up and forward. Here's an example of how thinking you are looping a belt or rope around your opponent's body and tying him up.

Here's the throw at the peak of its effect.

The momentum of the attack has its effect and Steve finishes the throw.

Steal Shoulder Hip Throw

Alan, on the right, is tied up with Chuck. Alan makes sure his body is outside of Chuck's left leg as shown.

Alan uses his left hand to pull Chuck's right elbow into his belly as Alan uses his right hand to hook under Chuck's left shoulder. As he does this, Alan uses his left foot to step across Chuck as shown.

Body Drop and Over Body Throws

Alan uses his right leg and foot to step across and in front of Chuck and positions his feet as shown. Alan uses his right hand to trap Chuck's left shoulder and his left to pull Chuck forward.

Alan rolls Chuck over his hip as shown.

Alan finishes by throwing Chuck flat on his back.

Throws and Takedowns

Knee Body Drop

This is an old throw, but is still effective. In judo, it's called Hiki Otoshi (Pulling Drop) and is one of the oldest forms of the Body Drop used in Japanese jujitsu.

Derrick (left) has positioned himself on the outside and left of Drew's body as shown. Derrick is leading with his left foot and has it placed near Drew's right foot. Derrick is positioned this way so he has room to move.

You can use any grip you choose, but Derrick is using his left hand to grab Drew's left lapel as he attacks. Derrick is using his left hand to pull on Drew's left sleeve at the elbow. Derrick pivots on his left foot as he swings his right leg wide and behind his body.

Body Drop and Over Body Throws

Derrick drops on his right knee as shown as he shoots his left leg across the front of Drew. Derrick's left leg is flexed with a bend in his knee (his left knee is pointed downward toward the mat) and his right heel is pointed up as shown. You can see how Derrick is low and under Drew's center of gravity.

This shows Derrick attacking Roman during randori (free practice) and using a double lapel grip.

Derrick uses both hands to pull Drew forward and to his left front corner. You can see how Derrick's left leg has blocked Drew's body and legs and is important in the action of the throw.

Derrick throws Drew and will immediately follow through to a ground attack.

Body Drop and Over Body Throws

2 on 1 Body Drop Front Takedown

You don't always have to throw your opponent onto his back and this takedown proves it. This throw was featured in my book CHAMPIONSHIP SAMBO: SUBMISISION HOLDS AND GROUNDFIGHTING.

Chris (left) is leading with his left foot as he grips Bob. This is a good example of what a takedown does; it gets your opponent to the mat for you to finish him.

Chris shucks off Bob's right hand and arm as he starts to shoot in for the attack.

Throws and Takedowns

Chris gets to the outside of Bob's body as shown as he uses the Russian 2 on 1 tie up, controlling Bob's right arm.

Chris moves in closer and sucks in Bob's right upper arm to his chest as shown. Chris uses his left shoulder and upper chest to drive down and forward, controlling Bob's right shoulder.

Chris uses his right arm to continue to hook under Bob's right arm and uses his left hand and arm to reach round Bob's hip and tightwaist him. As he does this, Chris moves his left him close to Bob's right hip.

324

Body Drop and Over Body Throws

Chris places his left foot in front of Bob as shown, making sure to flex his knee for maximum spring as he throws Bob forward. You can see how Chris is driving Bob directly forward.

Here's another view of how Chris drives Bob forward onto his front and his knees. Chris has taken Bob down and is ready to follow through with a submission technique.

Chris immediately follows through with an Armpit Lock and gets the tap out.

Throws and Takedowns

ABOUT THE AUTHOR

Steve Scott holds advanced black belt rank in both Kodokan Judo and Shingitai Jujitsu and is a member of the U.S. Sombo Association's Hall of Fame. He first stepped onto a mat in 1965 as a 12-year-old boy and has been training, competing and coaching since that time. He is the head coach and founder of the Welcome Mat Judo, Jujitsu and Sambo Club in Kansas City, Missouri where he has coached hundreds of national and international champions and medal winners in judo, sambo, sport jujitsu and submission grappling. Steve served as a national coach for USA Judo, Inc., the national governing body for the sport of judo as well as the U.S. Sombo Association and the Amateur Athletic Union in the sport of sambo. He also served as the coach education program director for many years with USA Judo, Inc. He has personally coached 3 World Sambo Champions, several Pan American Games Champions and a member of the U.S. Olympic Team. He served as the national team coach and director of development for the under-21 national judo team and coached U.S. teams at several World Championships in both judo and sambo. He was the U.S. women's team head coach for the 1983 Pan American Games in Caracas, Venezuela where his team won 4 golds and 6 silvers and the team championship. He also coached numerous U.S. teams at many international judo and sambo events. Steve conducted numerous national training camps in judo at the U.S. Olympic Training Centers in Colorado Springs, Colorado, Marquette, Michigan and Lakes Placid, New York. He also serves as a television commentator for a local MMA production and conducts submission grappling clinics for MMA fighters. As an athlete, he competed in judo and sambo, winning 2 gold medals and a bronze medal in the National AAU Sambo Championships, as well as several other medals in smaller national sambo events and has won numerous state and regional medals in that sport. He was a state and regional champion in judo and competed in numerous national championships as well. He has trained, competed and coached in North America, South America, Europe and Japan and has the opportunity to train with some of the top judo and sambo athletes and coaches in the world.

Steve is active in the Shingitai Jujitsu Association with his friend John Saylor (www.JohnSaylor-SJA.com) and has a strong Shingitai program at his Welcome Mat Judo, Jujitsu and Sambo Club. He has authored several other books published by Turtle Press including ARMLOCK ENCYCLOPEDIA, GRAPPLER'S BOOK OF STRANGLES AND CHOKES, VITAL LEGLOCKS, GROUNDFIGHTING PINS AND

BREAKDOWNS, DRILLS FOR GRAPPLERS and CHAMPIONSHIP SAMBO, as well as the DVD, CHAMPIONSHIP SAMBO. He has also authored COACHING ON THE MAT, SECRETS OF THE CROSS-BODY ARMLOCK (along with Bill West), THE JUJI GATAME HANDBOOK (along with Bill West), PRINCIPLES OF SHINGITAI JUJITSU (along with John Saylor) and THE MARTIAL ARTS TERMINOLOGY HANDBOOK, as well as the DVD, SECRETS OF THE CROSS-BODY ARMLOCK. Steve is also active in training law enforcement professionals with Law Enforcement and Security Trainers, Inc. (www.lesttrainers.com) and is a member of ILEETA (International Law Enforcement Educators and Trainers Association).

Steve is a graduate of the University of Missouri-Kansas City and teaches jujitsu, judo and sambo full-time as well as CPR and First-aid. For over thirty years, he worked as a community center director and coached judo, jujitsu and sambo in various community centers in the Kansas City area. He has conducted about 300 clinics and seminars across the United States and can be reached by e-mailing him at stevescottjudo@yahoo.com or going to www.WelcomeMatJudoClub.com. For many years, he was active as an athlete in the sport of Scottish Highland Games and was a national master's champion in that sport. He is married to Becky Scott, the first American woman to win a World Sambo Championship. Naturally, they met at a judo tournament in 1973 and have been together ever since.

Steve's first coach, Jerry Swett, told him as a teen-ager that he had a God-given gift for teaching and this impelled Steve to become a coach, and eventually, an author. Steve's second coach, Ken Regennitter, helped him start his judo club and loaned him the mat first mat ever used at the Welcome Mat Judo, Jujitsu and Sambo Club. Steve owes much to these kind men. His life's work and most satisfying accomplishment has been his effort as a coach to be a positive influence in the lives of many people.

Throws and Takedowns

Throws and Takedowns

Index

Symbols

1-Arm Knee Drop 160–166
2-Arm Tackle 287–289
2 on 1 Body Drop Front Takedown 323–325
2 on 1 Far Lapel Body Drop 311–313
2 on 1 Far Lapel Grip 46
2 on 1 Lapel Knee Drop 191–193
2 on 1 Near Lapel Grip 47
2 on 1 Shoulder Grip 41
2 on 1 sleeve grip 224
2 on 1 Tie Up 244

A

Ankle Pick to Toehold 137–140
Ankle Scoop Pick Up Throw 134–136
Arm Trap Body Drop 314–315
Arm Wrap Knee Drop 203–205

B

back grip 36, 270
Back Grip Body Drop 309–310
Back Grip Hip Throw 316–317
Back Grip Knee Drop 196–199
balance 20–23
Belly-to-Belly Throw 112–113
Belt Grip 37
Belt Grip Body Drop 309–310
block 59
Body Drop 302–308, 320–325
body drop throw 25, 26, 301
body lock 48
Both Arms Knee Drop 188–190
Both Hands Body Drop 304–305
both lapels grip 42
Both Sleeves (Arm In) Knee Drop 182–184
Both Sleeves (Arm Out) Knee Drop 185–187
both sleeves grip 42
bridge position 60
Buck 70–90
Buck (No Jacket) 76–79

C

center of gravity 52, 59, 63, 151
Chair Throw 70
control 16–17
counter grip 28
cross-body straight leglock 266
Cross Arms Knee Drop 173–177
Cross Body Outer Hook Throw (No Jacket) 232–233
Cross Body Outer Leg Hook 234–238, 242
Cross Body Outer Leg Hook (Double Lapel Grip) 237–238
Cross Body Outer Leg Hook (Lapel and Back Grip) 234–236
cross grip 45, 216, 283, 290
Cross Grip Major Outer Hook 274–275
Crotch Lift 141–145
Cuban Leg Grab (No Jacket) 118–119
Cuban Leg Grab (Using Jacket) 120–123
cut against the grain 64

D

defense 58–61
defensive grip 28
dominant grip 28, 29
double lapel grip 237, 321
drilling 27
duck under 287–288

E

evade 60, 64

F

Face First Knee Drop 206–209
Fireman's Carry 210–227
Fireman's Carry from a Cross Grip 216–218
Fireman's Carry Front Drop 214–215
Fireman's Carry Knee Drop 224–227
Fireman's Carry Shoulder Shoot 219–221
fitness 58
fitting in 24
floating elbow 30, 50
flop and drop 156
follow through 25
Foot Kick Throw 296–298
Foot Prop Throw 104–107
force 17
Front Double Leg 129–130
Front Takedown 323–325
Front Thigh Lift 98–101

G

grip 28–30, 30–32, 34, 55
grip fighting 29–31, 58

H

Hand Prop Throw 131–133
Hand Wheel 146–148
Head and Arm Knee Drop 201–202
high collar grip 49, 250, 302
hikite 29
Hiki Otoshi 320
Hip Block 61
Hip Throw 194, 316–319
Hopping Major Inner Hook 290–292
Hopping Outer Leg Hook Throw 270–273
hop around defense 59, 62

I

Inner Leg Hook 293–295
Inner Thigh Roll to Leglock 263–266
Inner Thigh Throw 95–97, 250–262
Inner Thigh Throw (Attack Opponent's Leg) 254–257
Inner Thigh Throw (High Collar Grip) 250–253
Inner Thigh Throw (Lapel and Back Grip) 258–259
Inner Thigh Throw from an Overhook 260–262
Inside Leg Hook Attack 98
Inside Thigh Lift 91–94
Ippon 241

J

jack up 163
judo 10, 15, 18
jujitsu 10

K

Kake 23
Kano, Prof. Jigoro 15
Kharbarelli Pick Up 91, 98
Knee Body Drop 320–322
Knee Drop 167–169
Knee Drop Throw 151–153, 170–172
Kodokan Judo 15
kumi kata 34
Kuzushi 23

L

lapel and back grip 234, 258
lapel and shoulder grip 38
Lapel and Sleeve Swing Knee Drop 178–181
leading hand 29

leglock 263, 266
leg grab 117, 286
leg hooks 231
leg jam 84
leg jam defense 63
leg lace 95–97
Leg Lace Throw 91–94
leg wrap 91–94
lifting hand 29
lifting throws 10, 69
looping grip 40, 98, 104
Looping Grip Knee Drop 198–200
Low Inside Thigh Lift 95–97

M

Major Inner Hook 98, 99, 287–289
Major Outer Hook 274–275
Metz 124–128
Minor Inner Hook 276–282
Minor Outer Hook 283–286
monster grip 36
Morote Seoi Nage 188
movement 58–59

N

neutral grip 28, 31, 34, 276

O

Open Chest Body Drop 306–308
Outer Hook from an Overhook 248–249
Outer Hook from the 2 on 1 Tie Up 244–247
Outer Leg Hook 267–269
Outer Thigh Sweep Throw 102–103
Outside Thigh Sweep 88
overhook grip 48, 248, 260
Over Body throws 301

P

pick ups 117
pistol grip 43
posture 52

power throws 11
project 19
pulling drop 320
pulling hand 29
pummeling 58

R

reap 231
rear throw 70
rotation 151
Russian 2 on 1 Grip 43, 44
Russian 2 on 1 grip 124, 287

S

safety 26
sag 59, 63
sambo 9, 10, 15, 69
shoulder grip 38, 170–172
Shoulder Throw 280–282
Shoulder Trap 46
Shoulder Wheel throw 210–213
Side Body Drop 314–315
Side Sweeping Hip Throw 242–243
single leg throw 118
Sliding Foot Sweep 108
sprawl 60, 65
square stance 56–57, 293
stability 151
stages of a throw 23
stance 51–57, 167
Steal Shoulder Hip Throw 318–319
steering hand 29, 30
sticky foot 296
stiff arm 267
sugar foot 53
sweep 231
Sweeping Hip Throw 80, 239–241
Sweeping Hip throw 242

T

Tai Otoshi 25
takedown 51
Thigh Lift 129–130
Thigh Sweep Throw 108–111

throw 51
tight waist 48, 70, 141, 245
Tight Waist (Hip Throw) Knee Drop
    194–195
timing 231
toehold 137, 139
Total Victory 241
Tsukuri 23
tsurite 29
turn out 60

U

uchikomi 27
Uchi Mata 95
underhook 46
Ura Nage 70

W

weight distribution 31
wrestling 112

Also Available from Turtle Press:
Drills for Grapplers
Vital Point Strikes
Groundfighting Pins and Breakdowns
Defensive Tactics
Secrets of Unarmed Gun Defenses
Point Blank Gun Defenses
Security Operations
Vital Leglocks
Boxing: Advanced Tactics and Strategies
Grappler's Guide to Strangles and Chokes
Fighter's Fact Book 2
The Armlock Encyclopedia
Championship Sambo
Complete Taekwondo Poomse
Martial Arts Injury Care and Prevention
Timing for Martial Arts
Strength and Power Training
Complete Kickboxing
Ultimate Flexibility
Boxing: A 12 Week Course
The Fighter's Body: An Owner's Manual
The Science of Takedowns, Throws and Grappling for Self-defense
Fighting Science
Martial Arts Instructor's Desk Reference
Solo Training
Solo Training 2
Fighter's Fact Book
Conceptual Self-defense
Martial Arts After 40
Warrior Speed
The Martial Arts Training Diary for Kids
Teaching Martial Arts
Combat Strategy
The Art of Harmony
Total MindBody Training
1,001 Ways to Motivate Yourself and Others
Ultimate Fitness through Martial Arts
Taekwondo Kyorugi: Olympic Style Sparring

For more information:
Turtle Press
1-800-77-TURTL
e-mail: orders@turtlepress.com

http://www.turtlepress.com